TYBEE ISLAND
The Long Branch of the South

This photograph of the Tybee Lighthouse was taken c. 1929. The building in the foreground is the Head Keepers Cottage. Built in 1881, it is one of the few Stick style houses on Tybee Island. The Second Assistant Keepers Cottage, on the left, was built in 1862 as a barracks for the Union soldiers who garrisoned Tybee during the Civil War. Note the attached kitchen on the rear of the building. (Tybee Island Historical Society.)

THE MAKING OF AMERICA

TYBEE ISLAND

The Long Branch of the South

ROBERT A. CIUCEVICH

ARCADIA

Copyright © 2005 by Robert A. Ciucevich.
ISBN 978-1-58973-086-1

Published by Arcadia Publishing,
Charleston SC, Chicago IL, Portsmouth NH, San Francisco CA

For all general information contact Arcadia Publishing at:
Telephone 843-853-2070
Fax 843-853-0044
E-Mail sales@arcadiapublishing.com
For customer service and orders:
Toll-Free 1-888-313-2665

Visit us on the Internet at www.arcadiapublishing.com

Built c. 1900 as a boarding house, the Collins Cottage (pictured here in the 1930s) on the Back River was operated by R. L. Bynum as the Riverside House until it was purchased in 1920 by John T. Collins, the author's great-grandfather, as a summer retreat. The Collins family summered at Tybee while John commuted to Savannah by train, and later car, to attend to business at his Collins Plumbing and Gas Fitting. Three generations of the Collins family—Ciucevichs, Grevemburgs, and Keatings—spent their summers here until the cottage passed out of the family in 1993. This book is for all of them.

CONTENTS

ACKNOWLEDGMENTS

Like all histories, this account of Tybee's past is the culmination of the work of several different authors and contributors—reporters, historians, novelists, essayists, and everyday citizens—this is their account as much as it is mine. The framework of much of this history is their contribution, for which I give my thanks and appreciation. In the same way that their work proved vital in the writing of this account, I hope someday that this book will provide a stable foundation for other historians to build on as well.

Although the works of several authors informed the writing of this book, I am particularly indebted to the following: Davis Hurst Thomas's *St. Catherines: An Island in Time*, which provided the basis for the sections of Chapter One dealing with Spanish Colonial Georgia and Florida; Ralston B. Lattimore's *Fort Pulaski National Monument: National Park Service Historical Handbook Series No. 18*, which provided the lion's share of source material for Chapter Two; and Randolph Mark's report for the Savannah District Corps of Engineers entitled "Fort Screven Historic, Environmental, and Cultural Assessment," which provided excellent descriptions of Fort Screven as well as an insightful analysis of its historic significance within a regional and national context. And finally, I would like to acknowledge Cynthia Miller's *Tybee Island, Ga.: Changing Images and Land Uses, 1733–1895*, which served as an early framework for the book through its insightful sketch of the island's developmental history from colonial times to the advent of the resort period.

Several people and organizations were instrumental in making this book possible. I would especially like to thank Cullen Chambers, executive director of the Tybee Island Historical Society, who graciously allowed access to the Society's ample photo and image collection; Sharon Lee, reference librarian at the Bull Street Branch of the Live Oak Public Libraries, who scanned several images from the library's Gamble Collection that appear in this book; and Mandi Johnson, visual materials archivist at the Georgia Historical Society, for her assistance in garnering several outstanding images from the GHS photo collection.

I would like to thank Arcadia Publishing and especially my editor, Jim Kempert, who did a great job with the manuscript and organizing the images. His sensitive and easy editing style made the completion of this book an enjoyable experience.

And of course, I would like to thank my wife Kara, and my family, for their patience and support.

INTRODUCTION

Night fell over Tybee Island. All afternoon, trains, creeping across the marshes and winding channels that separated the several islands from the mainland, had dumped week-end crowds under the Tybee station shed, from which point they deployed to beach homes, bath houses, the hotels or one of the pavilions. The breeze blowing in from the Atlantic picked up the smells of buttered popcorn, hamburgers, hot dogs, wet bath-house floors, and informed the arrivals they were there for a holiday.
—Harry Hervey, *The Damned Don't Cry*, 1939

Most Tybee Island residents would be surprised to learn that Tybee was at one time—a time not that long ago—one of the great seaside resort destinations of the south. Many of the older folks might recall fond memories of the Tybrisa Pavilion and maybe even Hotel Tybee, but few now really remember the magnitude and glory of the resort in its golden era of the 1920s and 1930s. Today, for the most part, Tybee's famous past has all but been forgotten.

Tybee is unique in Georgia as the only barrier island to be developed by a land development company as a coastal resort for the general population. Georgia's other barrier islands were owned by wealthy industrialists who built large residences to serve as retreats, such as "Dungeness" on Cumberland (built by Thomas Carnegie in the 1910s) and "Main House" on Ossabaw Island (built by the Torrey Family in 1924), and by land developers who constructed exclusive, elegant hotels such as the Cloister Hotel (*c.* 1928) on Sea Island and Jekyll Island Club Hotel (*c.* 1901) on Jekyll Island, as remote vacation destinations for the wealthy.

On Tybee however, the Ocean House (*c.* 1876) and Hotel Tybee (*c.* 1891) were built by the Tybee Improvement Company and the Tybee Beach Company, respectively, in an effort to attract the general population and to stimulate the sales of private building lots. Whereas Georgia's other barrier islands were kept intentionally remote, with steamer boats remaining the only means of access until well into the twentieth century, rail service was introduced to Tybee in 1887 in an effort to increase public accessibility and therefore visitation to the island. Unlike the architect-designed cottages of Jekyll Island, Tybee's simple frame cottages were built for middle class families—not just for Savannahians, but for Georgians from interior cities such as Atlanta, Augusta, and Macon, and later, the cities of Alabama and South Carolina as well. Its widespread popular appeal and subsequent development into a regional middle-class resort earned Tybee such names as "Georgia's Playground" and "The Queen of the South Atlantic Resorts."

Tybee also has the distinction of being the only example in Georgia, and perhaps on the entire south Atlantic coast, of the American coastal resort movement. The movement finds its roots in the English coastal resorts of Scarborough and Briton, whose bracing seawater and air were touted by eighteenth-century English physicians for the supposed virtues of their curative powers. By the early nineteenth century the idea was transplanted to America and gave rise to the coastal resorts along the Atlantic. Many Georgians and others throughout the south traveled north to Long Branch, New York; Cape May, New Jersey; and Nantucket, Rhode Island where resorts that had been in operation for many years set the standard with amenities such as established transportation networks, hotels, pavilions for dancing and picnics, service-oriented businesses, and amusement establishments. Tybee was modeled after these northern resorts and was even referred to in advertisements as "The Long Branch of the South." The resort continued to grow, and with the completion of the Tybee Road in 1923, the island had developed into one of the most popular summer beach resorts on the south Atlantic coast.

The purpose of this book is twofold: to provide an overall history of the island from its colonial beginnings to the present, and to record for the first time a comprehensive history of Tybee's development into a coastal resort. Over the years, while conducting research on Tybee's cottages and neighborhoods, I have noticed the need for an overall history of the island. Apart from a few short histories that date from the early twentieth century, there is no comprehensive history available that combines all the accepted—and suspect—accounts of the island's past. Parts of Tybee's colonial and antebellum history are relatively well known. There are scores of historic and modern accounts that outline the navigational and military importance of Tybee Island to the Savannah area. In addition, magazine and newspaper articles have provided small glimpses of Tybee's past—vignettes of Spanish and French colonial life, the establishment of the Tybee Lighthouse, tales of the Martello Tower, the siege and reduction of Fort Pulaski, the Big Band era and dances at the Tybrisa, and sentimental accounts of riding the train to Tybee to spend the day at the beach.

My intent was to combine all these colorful tales into one account, augmenting those parts of Tybee's history that are well known, and hopefully, filling in those parts that are not so well known. Tybee Island's development into a regional resort on a scale that rivaled the nation's most popular public beach resorts of the late Victorian period is one of the parts that is not very well known. I hope this book satisfies the need to preserve that history. While the first three chapters largely present an overview of information from various secondary sources, the rest of this book presents mostly new scholarship that chronicles the development of Tybee as a resort during the late nineteenth and early twentieth centuries, as well as its growth into a year-round community from the 1930s to the present.

Chapter One

FROM EARLY EXPLORERS
TO EARLY REPUBLIC

Although no known Native American settlement has ever been located on Tybee Island, the Guale Indians of coastal Georgia were undoubtedly among its earliest, albeit occasional, occupants, as the barrier islands were ideal hunting and fishing grounds. Indeed, the Guale were among the first indigenous people met by Europeans exploring north of Mexico. Lucas Vasquez de Ayllon encountered the Guale in 1520 during his exploration of the east coast of America, claiming for Spain the area from the Bahamas to Nova Scotia—later known as La Florida. Hernando De Soto's expedition through what is now the southeastern region of the United States encountered the Guale while crossing Georgia in 1540, and the French encountered them while establishing short-lived settlements on Port Royal Sound in what is now South Carolina in 1562 and at a strongpoint named Fort Caroline at the mouth of the St. John's River in Florida in 1563. After recapturing the region for Spain, Pedro Menendez de Aviles established the first permanent European settlement in North America at St. Augustine in 1565, which became the capital of the Spanish colony in northeast Florida.

Coastal Georgia as Part of the Province of Guale

The establishment of St. Augustine marked the beginning of a century-long period of Spanish colonization of the Guale and other Indian tribes. In an effort to protect Spain's new holdings, Menendez scouted out potential sites to establish mission outposts. In addition to converting the native population to Christianity, the Spanish crown used the missions, along with the presidios established at strategic points, as a pioneering frontier institution to occupy, settle, and hold its vast territory. Since Spain lacked a sufficient number of colonists, the goal of the mission system was to develop the local population into Spanish citizens and loyal subjects of the crown. In order to achieve this end, Menendez established a string of missions along the Georgia-Florida coast during the late sixteenth century. According to David Hurst Thomas in *St. Catherines: An Island in Time*, the seeds of Menendez's efforts later bore fruit: "at its seventeenth century zenith, La Florida consisted of about three-dozen missions, organized into two major branches, each originating in the colonial capital of St. Augustine and snaking out into the hinterlands." In all, about 70 Franciscan friars ministered to over 25,000 Native Americans. "To the west lived the Timucuan, Apalachee, and Apalachicola Indians; to the north [toward Tybee Island] lay the Province of Guale," according to Thomas. At least 10 missions were located within the present state of Georgia. During the "Golden Age" of the Georgia missions, a period lasting generally from 1605 to 1670, the Franciscan friars were very successful in converting thousands of Guale to Christianity, thus providing effective allies for the Spanish to defend La Florida against native and European threats.

The Spanish named the Guale Indians for the chiefdom centered at the principal town on the island of Guale, known today as St. Catherines Island, about 50 miles south of Tybee. The associated Franciscan mission that was established here during the sixteenth century became known as Santa Catalina de Guale. Although no mission is known to have existed on Tybee itself, the island was geographically part of the northern series of missions charged with the task of colonizing the Guale of coastal Georgia and securing the Georgia coast for Spain. Within the northern stretch of missions, Tybee was located between the mission of Santa Catalina de Guale and the town of Santa Elena, the second town established by Spain in North America, located on present-day Parris Island, South Carolina. Tybee was referred to by the Spanish as "Los Bajos," which means "the shoals." The Savannah River, which flows into the Atlantic at Tybee Roads, was referred to as "Rio Dulce," which means "sweet" or "salt" river. Tybee Roads was referred to as "Bahia de los Bajos," or "Bay of Shoals."

During the sixteenth and seventeenth centuries, Tybee Island was part of a territorial struggle between colonizing European powers jockeying for influence and control of the east coast of North America. Although Spain laid claim to coastal Georgia and its barrier islands, England and France consistently sought to undermine Spanish control of the area through alliances and trade agreements with local Native American tribes, military incursions, and eventually, colonization.

In 1586 the English pirate Francis Drake attacked the Georgia coast and burned St. Augustine. The attack led the Spanish to abandon their garrison at Santa Elena in 1587. The withdrawal from South Carolina made Santa Catalina de Guale on St. Catherines Island Spain's northernmost outpost. Tybee Island was now located outside the direct protection, and thus occupied holdings, of the Spanish mission chain. Spain's withdrawal from the immediate area encouraged other European powers to attempt to gain influence in the territory. In 1603 French traders came to Tybee to trade with the Guale, attracted by the abundance of sassafras that was native to the area. These French incursions resulted in a naval battle off Tybee between French and Spanish forces in 1605. Spain succeeded in defending its claim on Tybee and the northern coast of Georgia by defeating the French, in perhaps one of the first naval battles between European powers in North America.

Despite occasional incursions by the English and French, Spanish control of the region continued largely unchallenged throughout much of the seventeenth century until 1663 when Charles II of England awarded the territory of Carolina to several loyal backers. The Carolina grant angered the Spanish because the award not only included the Carolina and Georgia coasts south of the English Colony of Virginia, but extended to St. Augustine itself. Tensions were temporarily eased between the two European powers in 1670 through the Treaty of Madrid in which England and Spain agreed that actual possession of territory in North America, referred to as "the debatable lands," would determine ownership. Wasting little time in solidifying their claim, the English established a new settlement at Charles Town on the coast of Carolina in 1670. In response, Spain sent an expedition to destroy the new colony before it took root, although the attempt was thwarted by bad weather and high seas. In 1680, after a decade of encroachment into Spanish Guale from Charles Town, now the southernmost British settlement, a force of 300 English-led Yamasee Indians were sent to attack the principle town of Guale on St. Catherines Island. Although the invasion was repelled by a small garrison of Spanish soldiers and their neophyte Guale guards, Santa Catalina de Guale, the northernmost outpost of the Spanish missions in Georgia, was abandoned. As a result of the destructive raids of 1683–1685, the Spanish governor of Florida ordered the remaining missionaries and neophytes south of the St. Mary's River in 1686, thus ending the era of Spanish missions, and influence, in Georgia.

The English Colony of Georgia

Despite a few scattered attempts to form settlements on Tybee, the island remained largely uninhabited throughout the eighteenth and most of the nineteenth century. During this time the island was used primarily for governmental functions associated with navigation and defense.

The first known European attempt to settle on Tybee Island occurred during General James Oglethorpe's founding of Georgia in 1733. Oglethorpe planned a number of fortified, self-sufficient settlements on the outlying perimeter of Savannah. These villages would guard all overland and river-borne approaches to the colony. Because of the island's key location at the mouth of the Savannah

River, the settlement on Tybee was to be the colony's first line of defense against river-borne invasion.

In addition to building and manning a fort, Oglethorpe ordered the settlers to construct a navigational beacon on the north end of the island. Oglethorpe realized that if Savannah was going to prosper, the mouth of the river had to be clearly marked so that ships could easily find its entrance.

Little is known about the actual village that was built on Tybee because no plan or description of the settlement has been found. It is known that approximately 10 families inhabited the island and that individual lots were granted to the settlers in 1734. Each unmarried male received a 50-acre lot, while those with a wife and family received a 100-acre lot.

Tybee's soil proved incapable of supplying enough food to sustain the colony. Living conditions on the island were abysmal, due in large part to the fact that most of the lots were primarily marsh and wetland. The settlers' health began to fail, and by the end of 1734, half had died of disease. Because Oglethorpe and his officials did little to help the remaining settlers (instead attributing their problems to excessive drinking), all but one of the settlers were either dead or had abandoned the colony by 1735.

John Wesley, the father of Methodism, and his brother Charles first arrived in America in 1736 with General Oglethorpe, who was returning from England with new settlers and supplies for the new colony at Savannah. Wesley said his first prayer on American soil on a small hammock adjacent to Tybee, now known as Estill Hammock. In his journal, dated February 5, 1736, Wesley wrote: "We cast anchor near Tybee Island, where groves of pines running along the shore made an agreeable prospect, showing, as it were, the bloom of spring in the depth of winter." The next day, Wesley wrote: "We first set foot on American ground. It was a small uninhabited island over against Tybee. Mr. Oglethorpe led us to the rising ground, where we all kneeled down to give thanks."

Also in 1736, workers from Savannah under the direction of Noble Jones of Wormsloe, completed the work on the lighthouse that was begun by the settlers. The daymark (a lighthouse without a light) was octagonal in shape and constructed of brickwork and cedar piles. The beacon was 90 feet tall, making it the tallest structure of its kind in America at that time. It was also the first documented structure on Tybee.

In 1742 a second daymark was constructed to replace the first, which was swept away by a storm. This structure, built by Thomas Sumner, was 94 feet tall and had a flagstaff on top. In 1748 a full-time pilot was hired to assist ships coming down the river. Aside from the river pilot, Tybee remained uninhabited.

In accordance with an act permitting the importation of slaves into the colony, a lazaretto (pest house), or quarantine station, was erected on the westernmost tip of Tybee in 1768. Passing ships that had slaves or passengers aboard who were sick or infected with disease were left at the station's hospital to be treated before being allowed into the city. Those who died there were buried in unmarked graves in the hospital cemetery.

A third lighthouse was constructed in 1773 to replace the existing structure, which was again in danger of being washed away by the tides. This light was 100 feet tall, built of wood and brick, and was lit with spermaceti candles. This was Tybee's first true lighthouse.

Besides being the location of the lighthouse and quarantine station, Tybee served other purposes before the Revolutionary War. During the 1750s and 1760s, large tracts of land on the island were granted to seven individuals, most of whom were from the families of Carolina planters. According to Cynthia Miller in "Tybee Island, Georgia: Changing Images and Land Use, 1733–1895," these owners ran a cooperative horse pen on the island. Miller maintains that it was unlikely that the owners resided on the island since they all owned large estates elsewhere in Georgia. Slaves or servants most likely were left behind to tend to the horses. Following the Revolution, these tracts were confiscated by the state of Georgia because their owners had remained loyal to the English crown.

Tybee was a refuge for loyalists throughout the Revolutionary War years (1776–1782). Many loyalists and their families fled to the island to escape the mounting anti-crown sentiments and to avoid uncompromising persecution by the patriots who had gained influence in the city. A Tory settlement was soon established on the island in which merchants prospered from trade with the British ships anchored at the mouth of the Savannah in Tybee Roads.

In 1776, the royal governor of the colony, Sir James Wright, escaped to Tybee and was picked up by the British man-of war *Scarborough*. It was from ships moored off Cockspur Island that Governor Wright, other officials, and British sailors ventured to the Tory settlement on Tybee to take on supplies, relax, and spend time ashore. When the patriots realized that the settlement on Tybee was giving aid to the British, the Council of Safety gave the order for all houses on Tybee found to be sheltering British officers or Tories to be destroyed. A group of patriots led by Archibald Bulloch went in small boats to the island and destroyed the houses. Governor Wright, who was not ashore during the raid, gave an account of the incident in a letter he wrote aboard the *Scarborough* on March 26, 1776:

Yesterday an attempt was made on Tybee Island, where the Rebels expected to find me on shore, with several officers and gentlemen, but happily none were on shore from the ships, but four or five gentlemen belonging to the town, who happened to be there, they took and carried away—some marines were also on shore cutting wood and a ship carpenter was there one of which was killed and three wounded, so that it's thought that they cannot recover, and they burnt three dwellings houses.

Although no major battles occurred on Tybee during the Revolution, several other notable events did take place on the island. In July 1776, during the early days of the war, the first capture of a British vessel by an American commissioned warship was made off Tybee. In the spring of 1775 information was received by the patriots that a ship had set sail from London with a large cargo of gunpowder and ammunition intended for the use of the royalists in Savannah. Acting on this information, authorities in South Carolina dispatched a squadron of armed barges to intercept the powder ship before it entered Tybee Roads. The British, wary of anti-crown sentiments, dispatched an armed schooner to protect the powder ship, which lay off the coast of Tybee in anticipation of the ship's arrival. Meanwhile, the presence of the British schooner off Tybee prompted the provisional government of Georgia to act. A schooner was armed, commissioned, and placed under the joint command of Captain Bowen and Captain Joseph Habersham, who were instructed to either capture or run off the British schooner. Upon the approach of the American schooner the British stood out to sea, while the American sat in wait off Tybee.

On July 10, 1776, the British powder ship arrived off the coast of Tybee. Becoming aware of the American schooner, the powder ship abandoned its approach to Tybee Roads and put out to sea. The American schooner gave chase and, together with the armed barges from South Carolina, captured the ship and her cargo, 16,000 pounds of powder. Of the cargo captured, Georgia received a share of 9,000 pounds, 5,000 pounds of which were sent to the patriots near Boston and used in the Battle of Bunker Hill.

Despite the early efforts of the patriots, the British easily captured and occupied Savannah in December 1778. Shortly thereafter, the British built a small sand fort next to Tybee Light to guard the entrance to the Savannah River. Called Fort Tybee, the battery was sparsely garrisoned and consisted of only two artillery pieces: a 24-pounder cannon and a howitzer.

In 1779, at the request of American general Benjamin Lincoln, commander of the Southern Department of the Continental Army, the French naval commander Count Charles Henry d'Estaing set sail for Georgia to assist in the recapture of Savannah. During the weeks leading up to the Siege of Savannah, Tybee served as a major staging area for the French fleet, one of the largest gatherings of foreign ships every assembled off the coast of America.

On September 8, 1779, the French commander arrived off Tybee with a force consisting of a fleet of twenty line-of-battle ships, two 50-gun ships, eleven frigates, five small armed vessels, and 5,000 soldiers. A division composed of the *Artesian*, the *Fantasque*, the *Chimere*, the *La Blanche*, and the *Iphigenie* was detached from the fleet to advance and come to anchor a league and a half off the coast of Tybee. The following day d'Estaing, from the deck of the *Chimere*, directed the embarkation of 700 troops in long boats. When *Chimere*, along with three other frigates, crossed the bar of the Savannah River, a small English squadron stationed in Tybee Roads consisting of four ships, a galley, and several small craft weighed anchor and retreated upriver to Five Fathom Hole just below Savannah. The British at Fort Tybee began firing on the French vessels with little result. Once across the bar, the four French frigates came safely to anchor.

At nightfall d'Estaing ordered the debarkation of the troops aboard the frigates and directed the long boats to come alongside the *Chimere* in preparation for a landing on Tybee. Upon landing on the island, d'Estaing found that the British had evacuated. At daybreak the next day, September 10, d'Estaing, who had slept in the fort, ordered all the troops of the fleet landed on the north end of Tybee Island, and had them pass in review before him. That night he and his force re-embarked on their ships and sailed south to Ossabaw Sound.

On the night of September 12, a force of 1,200 French troops in long boats disembarked at Beaulieu, six leagues south of Savannah. After a two-week siege of the city, d'Estaing led a disastrous attack on the British lines on October 9, 1779. Shortly after their defeat at Savannah, Count d'Estaing and his remaining troops re-embarked upon their vessels and the French fleet set sail from Tybee for France. Although the combined French and American forces failed to liberate Savannah from the British during the Siege of Savannah, the French fleet succeeded in capturing several British vessels along the Georgia coast including the 50-gun ship *Experiment*, the 20-gun ship *Ariel*, four merchant ships, and several small sloops and schooners.

During the final months of the Revolution Tybee became the embarkation point for Georgia loyalists, soldiers, and government officials to board ships bound for the West Indies, Canada, and other British territories during the evacuation of Savannah in July 1782.

The Fledgling Nation

Following the Revolution, Tybee again lapsed into an uninhabited state. As in pre-colonial days, the island became known as a good place for hunting. Parties from Savannah and Carolina would arrive on Tybee to hunt deer, which were abundant on the island during the early nineteenth century. During the antebellum years Tybee's only inhabitants were the river pilots and lighthouse keepers. The quarantine station at the mouth of Lazaretto Creek, having fallen into disrepair, was abandoned in 1785 and a new station was built on Cockspur Island. The houses of a few river pilots and their families replaced the quarantine station at Lazaretto Point, while a few other houses were located at the hammock west of Chimney Creek, known today as Spanish Hammock.

After ratifying the Constitution in 1788, Georgia became a part of the United States. As a result, the state ceded the Tybee Lighthouse and its five-acre site to the U.S. government in 1790. The operation and maintenance of Tybee Light and the rest of the nation's navigational beacons were assigned to the U.S. Lighthouse Establishment. Upon assessing Tybee Light, it was determined that after 20 years of use the interior wood framing had reached a critical state of disrepair and would need to be replaced. To correct the situation, a requisition dated March 26, 1793 was sent from the office of George R. Putnam, commissioner of lighthouses, to George Washington in which a proposal was made for replacing the dilapidated woodwork. Since all matters great or small were directed to the nation's chief executive at the time, Washington, who apparently also acted as a de facto budget director as well, was presented with two estimates, "a hanging staircase for the sum of £160, or should a plain staircase be preferred for £110." As the fledgling nation had little in the way of a treasury, Putnam's requisition elicited the following response: "Approved with plain staircase. —G. Washington."

Tybee's remote location and uninhabited condition around the turn of the nineteenth century made it an ideal place for gentlemen to "settle their affairs of honor." In order to avoid their state's anti-dueling laws, South Carolinians would cross Calibogue Sound to Tybee where they would hold duels. The clearing around the lighthouse served as a dueling ground where numerous affairs were presumably settled. As J. H. Estill colorfully put it in his *c.* 1905 historical sketch "Tales of Tybee:"

> A fleet of big plantation canoes, with stalwart black slaves at the oars, and three or four gentlemen in the stern sheets, was a sign that there

would probably be something doing at Tybee that day and probably a funeral in Carolina the next.

The Martello Tower

During the War of 1812, it was feared that the British would again attack Savannah. The entrance of the river was unprotected, as there were no defensive works on Tybee at that time. There was, however, a system of early warning arranged with the keeper of Tybee lighthouse, who would warn of an approaching British fleet through a system of signals that could be seen at Fort Jackson and relayed to a man stationed in the cupola of the City Exchange, who would in turn give the warning to the city authorities if the enemy approached.

The British never came, but the experience brought attention to the need for some kind of coastal defense on Tybee. Around 1815, Isaiah Davenport was commissioned by the U.S. government to construct what came to be known as the Martello Tower.

A martello tower is a very strong, squat, round masonry tower developed by the British during the early nineteenth century as a type of coastal defense battery. Both the design and name were derived from a gun tower garrisoned by French troops at Mortella Point, Corsica, which had proven very effective in deterring the Royal Navy in 1794. The English were so impressed with the battery's defensive capabilities they erected a chain of 103 "martello towers" spaced one-quarter mile apart along the south and east coast of England between 1805–1812 to guard against the threat of invasion from Napoleon. The aim was to cover the most likely landing beaches and to hold the French until British reserves and Royal Navy ships could be rushed to the area. Following the War of 1812, the English erected 16 martello towers along the coast of British North America, principally along the Atlantic coast and Great Lakes areas of Canada, to guard against invasion from the fledgling United States. It appears the U.S. government was itself influenced by its British adversaries as several martello towers were built along the east coast of the United States during the 1810s and 1820s.

Tybee's Martello Tower was situated on the beach in front of the lighthouse. It was round and had thick tabby walls. In a letter written in 1861, John Screven, who was a principal owner of Tybee at that time, described the tower as "a tabby and wood structure 24 feet wide at the base, 34 feet tall with walls that were 11 feet 6 inches thick." As Tybee's Martello Tower was modeled after the English design, it featured most if not all of the common characteristics found in the English version (although the English towers were built of stone and brick, not tabby, a common building material used along the Georgia coast during the eighteenth and nineteenth centuries). The interior of English martello towers were divided into three stories: the ground floor served as the magazine where ammunition, stores, and provisions were kept; the first floor was the garrison's living quarters, which was generally divided into three or four rooms and featured fireplaces built into the walls for cooking and heating; and an interior stair lead from the garrison level to the roof or third floor, where the battery was situated. Surrounded by a four-foot parapet, a single 24-pounder cannon was situated in the center of the roof on a rotating carriage that could turn a full 360 degrees, allowing the gun to be fired in all directions. Loopholes in the parapet provided protection to defenders firing muskets. Martello towers were designed to accommodate a garrison of 24 men and one officer with each tower equipped with a cistern to provide clean drinking water. It appears that some modification of the original English design was made in the Tybee tower, in that it featured spaced openings in the wall that allowed muskets to be fired directly from platforms on the garrison level.

Like its English counterparts, the Martello Tower was designed to be mothballed in times of peace and garrisoned when the threat of invasion loomed. For several years a caretaker was stationed at the battery to ensure that it remained in proper repair, but eventually the tower was left to deteriorate. By the Civil War the tower was in a general state of disrepair, as noted by a war correspondent for the *New York Herald* who visited the Union troops garrisoned at the Martello Tower in 1862, shortly before the bombardment of Fort Pulaski. Along with the state of the fortification, the correspondent gave a thorough description:

> Within the battery rose the gray walls of a martello tower, showing but few evidences of decay, but within the platforms and floors, and the heavy timbers, were wasted by rot and rapidly crumbling to dust. It was a strange old tower, and a circular monument of ancient engineering skill. . . . When we reached the tower, Jack of the navy was engaged in rolling huge blocks of concrete into the lower door, and barricading it. Entrance to the tower is gained by a ladder of primitive style, which leads to a door 10 feet from the ground. Stepping upon a floor, rotten and dangerous, we gain a view of the internal arrangement of this curious work. In the center is a well constructed of heavy timber, which extends from a distance below the ground to the summit of the tower. At the bottom of this well was once a fine spring of water, but it had long since been clogged up with fallen timber and masses of concrete. From the well timbers are laid to the walls, and the flooring placed

upon them. The timbers are much decayed, and a large portion of the flooring has rotted and fallen in the dust. Two or three fireplaces, built in the walls, contained, when I saw them, a cheerful fire of hard pine. . . . With a little repair the work can be held for a long time against everything but artillery.

In what may be the first erroneous report of the origins of the tower, the *Herald* correspondent identified it as "an ancient Spanish Martello tower." Although constructed by the U.S. government, this type of battery was probably unfamiliar to many, as only a handful were built in the United States. The uniqueness of its design, its condition, and the use of tabby in its construction undoubtedly gave the fortification an exotic appearance, making it relatively easy to believe the structure was several hundred years old. The correspondent, with great flourish, went on to theorize the history of the fortification and the battles that occurred here:

> Evidently intended to resist a long siege, it showed that this was the scene of war and bloodshed generations ago. How many flags had waved over its gray battlements it were hard to tell. First the Spanish, then the French or English; afterwards the Colonial ensign; then the Stars and Stripes, followed for a brief time by a rebel flag of stars and bars, and now the ensign of the Union floats like a thing of beauty high above it.

In reality, Tybee's Martello Tower was not quite 50 years old at the advent of the Civil War, and had never been, nor would it ever be, tested in battle. This misinterpretation of the origins of the tower nevertheless persisted throughout the late nineteenth and early twentieth centuries, appearing in local newspapers and promotional literature for the new resorts.

Chapter Two

THE SIEGE OF FORT PULASKI

Shortly after South Carolina seceded from the Union in the winter of 1861, the state of Georgia began making its own preparations for secession and defense. In January 1861, just before officially leaving the Union, the governor of Georgia dispatched Colonel Alexander L. Lawton, commander of the 1st Regiment of Georgia Volunteers, to secure Forts Jackson and Pulaski, lightly guarded federal installations on the Savannah River that were yielded without a shot. Both brick forts were pivotal in the Confederacy's plans for the defense of Savannah. Centered on Fort Jackson, several small earthwork batteries were erected during the spring of 1861 along the inner waterways and around the city, forming an inner defense ring. Fort Pulaski, on Cockspur Island at the mouth of the Savannah, was the principal defense of Tybee Roads and the river approach to the city. In addition, small coastal batteries were erected on the outer islands and along the rivers and their approaches. The land defenses were complemented by a small fleet of riverboats, a "motley collection" of side-wheelers on which guns had been mounted. The "Georgia Navy," or "Mosquito Fleet," as the ragtag flotilla was known, was commanded by Commodore Josiah Tattnall, a renowned old naval officer who famously brought U.S. ships to the rescue of the British in Chinese waters with the battle cry "Blood is thicker than water."

On April 13, 1861, Confederate troops took possession of Tybee Island and erected a small earthwork battery around the Martello Tower, which served as a barracks for the troops. The battery was equipped with two eight-inch Columbiads to guard the entrance to the river. The post at Tybee was garrisoned first by the 1st Georgia Regulars under the command of Major William Duncan Smith, until July 17, 1861, when they were ordered to Virginia and were relieved by the 1st Volunteer Guard of Georgia under the command of Colonel Hugh W. Mercer.

In the summer of 1861, the Union had developed a plan to subjugate the South that included the naval blockade of key ports and the recapture of the southern coastal fortifications. On October 29, 1861 a combined Army and Navy expedition set sail from Hampton Roads, Virginia. Referred to as the "Great Expedition," the force included a squadron of 51 ships under the command of Captain Samuel F. DuPont and an invasion force of 12,500 men under the command of Brigadier General Thomas W. Sherman.

In November of 1861 the Union blockade reached Port Royal, South Carolina, just north of Savannah. The capture of Port Royal on November 7, 1861 rendered the garrison on Tybee and other outlying positions vulnerable to isolation and capture. Bracing for the impending invasion, fortifications at Fort Pulaski were increased. Brigadier-General Robert E. Lee, then the commander of Confederate forces in Georgia, South Carolina, and east Florida, arrived in Savannah shortly after the fall of Port Royal to inspect the defenses along the coast. Accompanied by Georgia governor Joseph E. Brown; General Alexander Lawton, commander of Savannah's land defenses; and Commodore Tattnall, the commander of the improvised Georgia Navy, General Lee surveyed the defenses at Fort Pulaski and made several suggestions to strengthen the fort, proclaiming that "it could withstand all the attacks of the enemy." As was widely held by the commanding officers of both sides, General Lee believed that Fort Pulaski was unassailable by sea or land.

Coupled with the devastating effectiveness of the Federal fleet in neutralizing the coastal earthwork batteries at Port Royal only days earlier, Fort Pulaski's perceived invincibility was a key factor in forming Lee's strategy for the city's defense. According to Ralston B. Lattimore in the National Park Service publication *Fort Pulaski*, Lee realized that without adequate naval support it would be impossible to defend the batteries along the sea islands, which were all within range of the Union gunboats, nor would it be possible to prevent the landing of Union troops without investing thousands of men—men who were badly needed in other theaters of the war. Believing that Fort Pulaski was a strong enough defense to keep Savannah secure, General Lee ordered the abandonment of the sea islands of Georgia, the removal of ordnance from the batteries, and the withdrawal of troops to the inner line of defenses on the mainland. As a result, Confederate forces on Tybee were evacuated on November 10, 1861. All of the batteries on Tybee were leveled and the heavy guns were removed to Fort Pulaski. Two companies of infantry assigned to the Tybee garrison were added to the complement at Fort Pulaski while the remaining troops were withdrawn to the mainland. Because Fort Pulaski was believed to be invulnerable to bombardment from Tybee, the island was left undefended.

Following the Battle of Port Royal Sound, Union patrols of the Georgia and Carolina coasts were becoming more effective in enforcing the naval blockade of the South. On November 13, 1861, the British steamer *Fingal*, carrying a cargo of munitions, ordnance, and other supplies, was the last ship to run the blockade into Savannah. In order to further strengthen the blockade of the city, Captain DuPont ordered the sinking of vessels laden with stone across the river channel and placed gunboats in Ossabaw and Warsaw Sound to prevent commercial or military vessels from entering or leaving the port through these back passages.

From his headquarters on Hilton Head Island, General Sherman contemplated his next move. He briefly considered bypassing Fort Pulaski and directly attacking the city of Savannah from behind, but ruled out this approach when it was deemed impractical from a logistical standpoint. Sherman's other options were to take Fort Pulaski by force or to wait for the garrison's food supply to run out. Deciding to explore the former, Sherman ordered his chief engineer, Captain Quincy A. Gillmore, to assess the practicality of reducing Fort Pulaski from Tybee Island. After a reconnaissance from Tybee on December 1, 1861, Gillmore concluded that it was possible for the fort to be reduced from Tybee using mortars and a new weapon, the rifled gun, which the Army had begun experimenting with in 1859. Gillmore drew up a plan for the siege of Fort Pulaski based on his knowledge of the preliminary test records of this new weapon. General Sherman approved Gilmore's plan with some reservations, stating for the record that he doubted the usefulness of rifled guns "until their effects could be fully tested."

In 1862, Gillmore's plan for the siege and reduction of Fort Pulaski was certainly considered radical as it defied tradition and the accepted military strategy of the day. In formulating such a daring plan, Gillmore risked the ridicule of his colleagues, who undoubtedly saw the plan as reckless and futile. At the time, Fort Pulaski was thought unassailable for several reasons. As detailed by Ralston B. Lattimore, its seven-and-a-half-foot thick, solid brick walls were impervious to long range bombardment from contemporary ordnance, and navy ships could not safely come within effective range of the fort without risking the concentrated fire of Pulaski's two tiers of guns. Because Pulaski was surrounded on all sides by the "broad Savannah River and wide swampy marshes," there was no firm ground to erect batteries nearer than Tybee, a distance of one to one-and-a-half miles away. As it was generally accepted that smoothbore guns and mortars did not possess the capability to breach heavy masonry walls beyond a distance of 700 yards, contemporary military thought dictated that erecting batteries on Tybee Island would serve as little more than a preamble to a direct assault.

In fact, it appears that long-range bombardment from Tybee was expected by the Confederate war department. In early January 1861, three months before the siege of the fort, General Lee, while inspecting Fort Pulaski's defenses for the third time that winter, stood on the parapet of the fort with Colonel Olmstead, pointed toward Goat Point on Tybee Island, and remarked, "Colonel, they will make it pretty warm for you here with shells, but they cannot breach your walls at that distance." While the long-range bombardment of Pulaski was probably expected, the devastating effectiveness of rifled guns on the masonry walls from such a distance could not have been predicted.

On December 4, 1861, General Sherman submitted Gillmore's plan to Washington and requisitioned siege guns for the proposed attack on Fort Pulaski. Shortly thereafter, scarcely more than three weeks after the Confederate withdrawal from the coast, Union troops occupied Tybee Island. The Tybee Light Station was made the base of operations for the siege of the fort, which became the Headquarters of the 46th New York State Volunteers. Temporary barracks were built on the lighthouse grounds and defensive positions were taken up around the Martello Tower, which was refortified with earthwork batteries.

Efforts toward the final investment of Fort Pulaski were begun in mid February. Before Gillmore's plan could be implemented, it would be necessary to isolate the fort by cutting off communication and supplies between it and Savannah. An effective blockade of the river was begun on February 11 when a battery of heavy guns, called Fort Vulcan, was secretly erected at Venus Point on Jones Island, on the north bank of the Savannah River. On February 13 the Confederate supply ship *Ida*, on one of its regular trips to the fort, was bombarded by the heavy guns of Fort Vulcan. Although the *Ida* managed to run the gauntlet unscathed, it would be its last trip to Pulaski. By February 15, the isolation of the fort was complete. A second strong battery, called Fort Hamilton, was erected at the western head of Bird Island on the south bank of the Savannah, opposite Fort Vulcan. At the same time, the telegraph wire between Savannah and Cockspur Island was destroyed. At this point neither supplies nor reinforcements could be brought to the fort, nor could its garrison escape to the mainland. The only communication with Savannah after this time was by couriers, who were forced to travel through the marshes at night to avoid the Union pickets.

With the fort now completely isolated, General Sherman sent Gillmore, recently promoted to brigadier general, to Tybee Island on February 19 to take command of all troops and to prepare for the bombardment of Fort Pulaski. On February 21 ordnance began to arrive in Tybee Roads and on February 27, work on constructing the earthwork batteries were begun.

During the next six weeks, from late February until early April, 1862, Tybee was the scene of intense preparation as Union troops undertook the grueling task of transporting materials, supplies, ammunition, and ordnance through the surf and across distances of one to three miles over sand and marsh. Gun emplacements, magazines, and bomb-proof shelters were built and a road over a mile long was constructed over swampy marsh using fascines in order to prevent heavy ordnance from sinking in the mud. A series of 11 earthwork batteries, mounting 36 guns in all, were constructed that extended a mile and a half along the north coast of Tybee from Goat Point at the mouth of Lazaretto Creek eastward almost to the lighthouse. As detailed in the April 19, 1862 edition of the *New York Daily Tribune,* the batteries:

> were all earthworks, revetted with sods, fascines, or hurdles, having parapets not less than eight feet in height, with traverses between the guns, deep and narrow embrasures, splinter-proofs for all the advanced works, capable of holding two reliefs of gunners off duty, and one or two service magazines in each battery.

Most of the work of constructing the earthen batteries was conducted at night, as the last mile of shore on which seven of the major batteries had to be constructed was in open view of Fort Pulaski and within range of its guns. The men were not permitted to speak above a whisper and before each morning the previous night's work was concealed through camouflage. Some of the most backbreaking work involved the transport of the heavy ordnance from the landing site near the lighthouse to the batteries nearly two miles away. Weighing up to 17,000 pounds each, it took nearly 250 men harnessed to a sling cart to haul each of the 36 pieces across the marsh to the gun emplacements.

For the Union troops garrisoned on Tybee during this time, life was difficult but apparently not unbearable. In *A Present for Mr. Lincoln: The Story of Savannah from Secession to Sherman*, Alexander A. Lawrence quotes a letter from a soldier in the 7th Connecticut Volunteers that provides a glimpse of the daily life of the soldiers on Tybee during this time:

> Pulaski shoots at us occasionally and the boys rather like it; for no one gets hurt, and relics accumulate; earthworks slowly rise; a gun gets mounted frequently; fleas bite continually; once in a while a mail comes in; somebody shoots an otter or eagle; teams and mulecarts work eighteen hours a day, drawing great loads of shot and shell two miles; and the beach is strewn with all the implements of war.

Meanwhile, while Union forces were preparing for battle, the Confederate garrison of 385 men stationed at Fort Pulaski was feeling the effects of isolation. Following the complete containment of the fort on February 15, Pulaski's only communication with the mainland was via an occasional mail brought in by courier through the marshes. Of the five companies stationed at Pulaski, four were from Savannah: Company B of the Oglethorpe Guard, the Washington Volunteers, the Montgomery Guard, and the German Volunteers. According to Lawrence in *A Gift for Mr. Lincoln*, the men were hopeful that help would soon arrive from the mainland. Edward W. Drummond, a Confederate soldier of the garrison, wrote in late March, "there is a prospect of our soon being set free again as our friends in Savannah are using every effort to drive the Yankees from our midst."

Drummond was referring to the construction of a floating battery that was then under construction in Savannah that General Lawton hoped would serve to "open communication with Fort Pulaski" and give "relief to our brother soldiers now confined in the Fort." Many of the men feared that relief would not arrive soon enough, as they were aware of the construction of the batteries along the north coast of Tybee. In the same letter dated late March 1862, Edward Drummond wrote, "they now have a string of Batteries along Tybee Beach . . . and are no doubt contemplating the destruction of this fort."

Despite the belief that the thick brick walls of the fort could not be breached by guns and mortars from the distance of the batteries on Tybee, the garrison at Fort Pulaski worked tirelessly during this period of isolation to prepare for what they expected to be a long siege. The men knew that as long as the fort's walls withstood the bombardment they could wait out the enemy for several months, as the fort had been provisioned on January 28 with a six-month supply of food, which with careful rationing could be made to last until mid-August or September.

On April 9, the day before the siege, Confederate General Lawton, unaware of the final preparations being made on Tybee, assigned an officer to serve on the newly completed floating battery intended to counter the blockade of Fort Pulaski from the mainland. The battery would never be used for its intended purpose.

Fort Pulaski is Fallen

On the morning of April 10, 1862, the dunes in front of the Union batteries were leveled and the guns were in plain view of the defenders in the fort. Soon after daylight, General Hunter, who had recently replaced General Sherman as commander of the Department of the South, sent Lieutenant Wilson, under a flag of truce, with the following written demand for the surrender of Fort Pulaski:

> To the Commanding Officer, Fort Pulaski:
>
> Sir: I hereby demand of you the immediate surrender and restoration of Fort Pulaski to the authority and possession of the United States. This demand is made with a view to avoiding, if possible, the effusion of blood which must result from the bombardment and attack now in readiness to be opened. The number, caliber, and completeness of the batteries surrounding you leave no doubt as to what must result in case of your refusal, and as the defense, however obstinate, must succumb to the assailing force at my disposal, it is hoped that you may see fit to avert the useless waste of life. This communication will be carried to you under a flag of truce by Lieut. J. H. Wilson, United States Army, who is authorized to wait any period not exceeding thirty minutes from delivery for your answer.
>
> I have the honor to be, Sir, very respectfully your most obedient servant,
>
> David Hunter Maj-Gen. Com'g.

Colonel Olmstead immediately responded to Hunter's demand with the following communication:

> To Maj-Gen. David Hunter, Commanding on Tybee Island.
>
> Sir: I have to acknowledge receipt of your communication of this date, demanding the unconditional surrender of Fort Pulaski. In reply, I can only say that I am here to defend the Fort, not to surrender it.
>
> I have the honor to be, very respectfully, your obedient Servant,
>
> Chas H. Olmstead, Col. 1st Vol. Regt. Of Georgia, Com'g Post

Having received Colonel Olmstead's reply, General Hunter gave the order to open fire at 8:10 a.m. Fire from both sides ensued, with volleys becoming increasingly rapid in their succession and accuracy. Throughout the day, the fire from Pulaski was largely ineffectual, as most shells either arced over the earthwork batteries or were buried in the sand revetments in front of the gun emplacements. The effect of the Union batteries on the walls of the fort was more successful, although the outcome of the first day of the siege was uncertain. A reporter for the *New York Daily Tribune* gave the following eyewitness account from the perspective of the troops stationed on Tybee:

At twelve, forty-one scars were counted on the south flank, the panacope and the south-east face of the fort, and several of the embrasures were considerably enlarged. During the afternoon fire slackened from both sides, and after sunset not more than seven or eight shells an hour were thrown till daylight the next morning. When I left the shore where I had witnessed the bombardment during the day, the fort, not withstanding its dents and scars, looked nearly as solid and capable of resistance as when fire was opened in the morning. It was not considered that the day's work had greatly hastened the surrender, the mortars having proved a disappointment, and the effect of the breaching fire being not yet sufficiently decided.

From their vantage point on Tybee, the attackers could not have known how successful the fire from the rifled guns had been that day in creating a breach in the fort's thick brick walls. On inspecting the exterior walls of the fort that night, Colonel Olmstead found the damage "worse than disheartening." He observed that at the southeast angle of the fort the wall was almost entirely shot away, to a depth of two to four feet, at one point revealing the interior of the casement. In addition, his ability to return fire on the batteries had been greatly diminished as nearly all the barbette guns and mortars bearing on Tybee had been dismounted and only two of the five casement guns were operational.

At daylight the next morning, Friday, April 11, the bombardment began again, with Fort Pulaski returning fire from some guns that had been remounted and repaired overnight. The Union batteries continued to bombard the southeast angle of the fort and within two hours a breach had been opened. By noon two great holes had been opened through the walls and the inside of the fort was visible from Tybee. It was apparent that the whole east angle of the fort would soon be in ruins. At the fort, shells from the rifle batteries were passing through the breach and striking the walls of the north magazine in which 40,000 pounds of black powder was stored. Fearing that the magazine would soon be compromised and the resulting explosion would end in the loss of many of the men under his command, Colonel Olmstead had little recourse other than surrender. At approximately 2:00 p.m. the Confederate flag was lowered and the white flag of surrender was raised.

When word of the fall of Fort Pulaski reached the northern states, it was front-page news. The headline of the Saturday, April 19, 1862 edition of the *New York Daily Tribune* read "SURRENDER OF FORT PULASKI—DETAILS OF THE BOMBARDMENT—TERRIFIC EFFECTS OF OUR FIRE—Union Loss One Killed and One Slightly Wounded—Rebel Loss

Three Wounded and 385 Prisoners." The *Tribune's* special correspondent at the siege submitted a report written on the day of the surrender, April 12, 1864, expressing jubilant surprise at the success of the siege on a fortification believed by both sides invincible:

> Two months of preparation, thirty hours of cannonading, and Fort Pulaski is fallen. It was one of the strongest works in the United States; perhaps the strongest but two. Indeed it was considered by many of the best Engineers in the service practically unassailable, and the most positive opinions were given against any attempt at its reduction. One officer of high reputation said there was not enough shot and shell in the country to make an impression on it; another said that the place would be as strong in the end of a month's bombardment as it was in the beginning; and the Chief of Engineers of the Regular Army put the climax to all statements by declaring that you might as well cannonade the Rocky Mountains as Fort Pulaski.

The significance of the Siege of Fort Pulaski cannot be underemphasized. The devastating success of the rifled gun in breaching the masonry walls of the fort was unprecedented, rendering these types of defenses obsolete. In his report to the secretary of war, General Hunter declared that:

> The result of this bombardment must cause a change in the construction of fortifications as radical as that foreshadowed in naval architecture by the conflict between the *Monitor* and the *Merrimac*. No work of stone or brick can resist the impact of rifled artillery of heavy caliber.

Although Union forces had gained control of Fort Pulaski and the outlying islands, Savannah would elude capture until December of 1864, when General Sherman presented the city as a Christmas gift to President Lincoln at the culmination of his famous "March to the Sea."

Following the end of the Civil War, Tybee remained occupied by Union troops until 1867. During that time, efforts were being made by the U.S. Lighthouse Establishment to repair or rebuild lighthouses that had been destroyed or disabled during the war by the Confederate government to prevent their use by Union forces. In 1862 a raiding party of the Montgomery Guards from Fort Pulaski destroyed a major portion of the Tybee Lighthouse by igniting a keg of powder on the third floor of the tower. The Lighthouse Establishment decided to rebuild the lighthouse utilizing the lower 60 feet of the old structure that remained standing. The new lighthouse (which still stands today) was completed in 1867 and is a completely fireproof, 150-foot tall tower constructed of masonry and metal. A cast iron and glass cupola at the top of the tower houses the lighthouse's first order Fresnel lens, which magnifies the light output of a 750 watt bulb to 30,000 candlepower, making it visible for 18 miles.

Chapter Three

FORT SCREVEN AND THE WIDER WORLD

As part of a nationwide effort to improve coastal defenses, the U.S. Army Corps of Engineers announced plans for the construction of a new fort on Tybee in 1872. In 1875, 205 acres were acquired by the federal government on the north end of the island for the establishment of a military reservation. The northern end of Tybee was chosen because of its historically recognized strategic location for the defense of Tybee Roads, Calibogue Sound, and the city of Savannah. Fort Screven, an Endicott Period or "Fourth Order" fort, was one segment of a network of coastal defense batteries conceived during the period of Caribbean and Pan American unrest of the 1890s and constructed along the Atlantic and Gulf coasts to protect major cities and ports from naval bombardment and blockade. The need for a stronger coastal defense system was necessitated by a dramatic change in U.S. foreign policy during the late nineteenth and early twentieth centuries in which America evolved from an isolationist country into a world power. Renewed resolve to enforce the Monroe Doctrine—a policy stating that the United States would regard as an unfriendly act any attempt by a European nation to interfere in the affairs of American republics or to increase colonial possessions in the Western Hemisphere—was demonstrated in 1895 through U.S. political intervention in British affairs in Venezuela and again through U.S. political involvement in the Cuban Revolution. As tensions mounted over the situation in Cuba, the United States prepared for war. A new battleship navy was quickly completed and in 1897 the implementation of a new system of coastal defenses was begun.

A Vast, Open Park Space

Because Savannah was one of the most important ports on the south Atlantic coast at the time (and the world's principal port for the export of cotton and naval stores), the War Department determined the construction of a new installation on Tybee Island to protect the entrance to the Savannah River a high priority. The first phase of Fort Screven was constructed from 1897 to 1904 as an Army coast artillery station. Originally called Fort Tybee, the name was later changed to Fort Graham after Brigadier General Montrose Graham, commander of Atlantic coast defenses. The plan for the post included four distinct sections that were separated by function and arranged by military hierarchy: a battery consisting of six poured-in-place, reinforced concrete gun emplacements; an officer's row of housing and headquarters buildings; a fort village including a senior non-commissioned officers row of housing, non-commissioned officers housing, enlisted men's barracks, and post service buildings; and a quartermaster's area including storage, service, and office buildings. The fort also included a post hospital, a regimental parade ground, and landscaped grounds with open space, streets, and pedestrian paths.

The battery area of the fort wrapped around the coastline of the northern end of the island, forming a U around the five-acre Tybee Lighthouse Station. The six gun emplacements that make up the battery were erected by the Venable Construction Company from 1897 to 1900. Each emplacement featured its own set of catwalks and corridors that led to the ammunition magazine below. The batteries were buttressed on the sea side by large sand dunes and sand embankments to conceal their location and to serve as added protection for the magazine. Ammunition for the guns was raised to the firing platform by an elevator and crew members used carts to wheel the shells to the guns.

Battery Brumby, the largest of the battery complexes, was the first to be completed and the only one in service during the Spanish American War, which only lasted eight months from April to November 1898. Begun in April 1897 and completed in July 1898, Battery Brumby featured four eight-inch rifles mounted on Buffington Crozier disappearing carriages and was manned by 4 officers and 157 men. On March 18, 1898, six weeks before Congress declared war on Spain, Fort Graham was officially commissioned as a military post and was renamed Fort Screven for Brigadier General James Screven of the Georgia Militia, a hero of the American Revolution. Fort Screven was garrisoned by Battery F of the 1st Coast Artillery, Company H of the 5th Infantry, and units of the Georgia Militia. In November 1899, after additional post buildings and batteries were completed, the troop strength at Fort Screven was increased by 180 men with the arrival of Battery C, 2nd Coast Artillery.

As the majority of the batteries at Fort Screven were still under construction during the Spanish American War, Savannah's coastal defenses were augmented by an electronic minefield deployed in the north channel of the Savannah River and by the U.S.S *Amphitrite*, which patrolled between Savannah and Charleston.

The minefield was operated by a small garrison stationed in the demilune area of Fort Pulaski. Each mine was attached to a buoy. A signal was transmitted to the garrison at Fort Pulaksi each time a ship struck a buoy. From their vantage point on Cockspur Island, the observers at Fort Pulaski could determine whether the ship was an enemy vessel and if so could electronically detonate the mines to prevent it from entering the channel.

Stationed at Port Royal, the *Amphitrite* was a double turreted monitor approximately 262 feet long and 55 feet wide with armaments that included four 10 inch guns, two mounted forward of the bridge and two aft. Built in 1874 and refurbished in 1895, the *Amphitrite* had an average speed of 12 knots and carried 13 officers and 200 men.

Construction of the remainder of Fort Screven's batteries continued during the Spanish American War, with the majority placed in service shortly after the end of the conflict in late 1898. Completed in March of 1899, Battery Garland, the easternmost battery directly overlooking the sea entrance to Tybee Roads, housed a single twelve-inch, long range rifle manned by 2 officers and 47 men. Battery Fenwick, on the opposite side of Battery Brumby, featured another single twelve-inch, long range rifle. Battery Backus, partially completed in September of 1898, featured three emplacements for 3.7-inch rifles on pedestal carriages when completed in 1900. This battery was oriented in a northerly direction and was intended, along with Battery Gant, to control the minefield area in Tybee Roads. Battery Gant, completed in February 1900 (although its guns were not mounted until 1903), carried two three-inch rifles on pedestal carriages in a parapet mount and was manned by a single officer and 25 men. Battery Habersham, completed in June 1900, was an M-shaped battery that contained eight twelve-inch mortars. Placed inland and to the west of the other batteries, which were located along the coastline, Battery Habersham contained the fort's greatest medium- and long-range firepower. The mortars were divided into two groups of four and were separated by thick, reinforced-concrete bunkers that housed the magazines. On each side of the battery, atop the magazines, stairs led up to two rounded observation towers that served as spotting platforms for the fire control officers. Manned by 7 officers and 219 men, Battery Habersham was by far the most complicated to operate.

In addition to the batteries on Tybee, a small, poured-in-place, reinforced-concrete battery like those at Fort Screven was erected near Fort Pulaski on the north shore of Cockspur Island to protect the north channel of the Savannah River. Begun in June 1899, Battery Hambright featured emplacements for two three-inch rapid fire guns.

The stark, functional, military character of the battery area of Fort Screven stood in sharp contrast to the rest of the post. Fort Screven was constructed at the same time that Tybee was developing as a popular summer beach resort, and as a result, the landscape plan for the fort as well as the vernacular military architecture of the buildings reflected the picturesque seaside location of the post. Influenced by the Renaissance and Baroque "grand" landscape planning concepts that were re-introduced on a national scale at the 1893 World's Columbian Exposition in Chicago, the same event that would later serve as a catalyst for the City Beautiful Movement of the late nineteenth and early twentieth centuries, Fort Screven represents an early adaptation of these concepts and as such was planned by the U.S. Army Corp of Engineers as a functional yet picturesque military landscape.

The highest expression of these concepts can be seen in the landscape design and military architecture of Officer's Row, a linear complex of buildings situated atop a 16-foot high, half-mile long, crescent shaped earthen berm overlooking the reviewing ground and the ocean. Consisting of the regimental headquarters, officers' club, officers' mess, and officers' quarters, the vernacular military classicism of the buildings, particularly the ranking officers' quarters, combined with its magnificent seaside setting, was unique for military posts in the southeastern region. The officers' quarters as a group were indicative of the army's aspirations for its ranking officers. Designed in an ordered, vernacular military expression of the Free Classic Queen Anne style (in this case an austere blend of Queen Anne and Colonial Revival styles), the houses that make up Officers Row were "grand in scale and design and gracious in living accommodations and material finishes." The ranking officers' quarters were characterized as frame, two-and-a-half story residences with deep, two story wraparound porches that extend around three sides and are supported by square, Doric columns.

These houses were exceptional examples of turn-of-the-century military housing and were reserved for the most senior of ranking officers at Fort Screven: the post commandant (building no. 38), the training officer (building no. 39), operations officer (building no. 40), and post chaplain (building no. 41). However, as put forth by architectural historian Randolph Marks in a report prepared for the Savannah District Corps of Engineers entitled "Fort Screven Historic, Environmental, and Cultural Assessment," the strength of Officer's Row did not lie solely in the individual character of its buildings, but as "a design concept [that] is magnified by its location atop the crescent-shaped berm that gathers the great open space before it into a unified and grand planning composition." Marks adds that the design concepts and planning similarities between Frederick Law Olmstead's Court of Honor at the Columbian Exposition, which served as one of the principal models for the City Beautiful Movement with its "great shoreline park surrounded by white classical buildings fronting onto Lake Michigan," and Officers Row, is very strong, noting Officer's Row's "equally grand, white military architecture located on a well-landscaped, crescent-shaped berm fronting onto a vast, open park space overlooking the Atlantic Ocean."

The original plan for the rest of the post also incorporated the same concepts of landscape planning found in Officer's Row, but to a lesser degree. The fort village area and, to some extent, the quartermaster's area, featured open space, tree groves, landscaped grounds, pedestrian paths, and curved roadways. The open areas were intended to be used for temporary military functions such as tent areas, parade grounds, rifle ranges, etc., but since these areas were not continuously in use, they also served as open space that provided vistas and allowed the flow of ocean breezes through the inland areas of the fort. Overall, military hierarchy determined the allocation of the prime beach side of the parade ground to the top ranking officers and their staff functions (Officer's Row) and the inland side to the enlisted men's barracks, the senior NCO Row, and service-related functions of the fort village area. These two linear development patterns were separated by the parade ground on the south but connected by a major east-west pedestrian walkway that extended from the rear of the regimental headquarters building to the quartermaster's area.

In addition to the senior NCO quarters and enlisted men's barracks, the fort village area also consisted of mess halls, latrines, the post exchange, and the serviceman's club. Several additional support buildings including a post office, library, bakery, gymnasium, chapel, bowling alley, field house, laundry, and fire station were added to the village as the post expanded during the 1910s and 1920s. The architecture of the buildings in the village is best characterized as military vernacular, having been designed by the Corps of Engineers for the semi-tropical climate of the Georgia coast. Although relatively unadorned, most of the buildings featured design elements such as overhanging eaves with shaped, exposed rafter ends, slate roofing tiles, and in some cases, one and two story galleried porches supported by plain, square columns. Some of the more substantial buildings, such as the massive enlisted men's barracks, the two-story quarters of the senior NCO Row, and the guard house exhibited vague elements of such popular early twentieth century styles as Queen Anne, Folk Victorian, Neoclassical Revival, and Colonial Revival.

The quartermaster's area, located the farthest from the coast, consisted of both permanent and temporary buildings designed for all types of storage and service functions. Most of these buildings, particularly the temporary ones, displayed a functional design with little or no ornament. Most were long, one story rectangular buildings with clapboard siding and slate-covered gable roofs. The more substantial permanent buildings, such as the quartermasters' offices and commissary building, featured subdued Folk Victorian–inspired ornamentation similar to that in the village, such as overhanging eaves with shaped, exposed rafter ends and round Tuscan columns. The quartermaster's area included a utility yard and saw mill as well as a stable, blacksmith shop, several service and repair shops, and various warehouses and storage sheds.

The completion of Fort Screven's initial phase of construction in early 1900 coincided with the nation's emergence as an international power, underscoring the necessity to maintain a strong coastal defense. The United States's willingness to protect its interests in Central and South America by enforcing the Monroe Doctrine created tensions with European nations that still had colonial possessions in the Western Hemisphere. As a result, coast artillery posts like Fort Screven were kept in a state of constant readiness during the 1900s to repulse any attacks by foreign navies. At the same time the need to defend distant holdings, such as the Philippines and Puerto Rico, increased as a result of the war with Spain and made it necessary to build up and maintain a strong naval presence in the world. In 1901, successful intervention in the Panamanian rebellion lead to an agreement with the new government that allowed the United States to build the Panama Canal. By 1904 America's "White Fleet" was one of the most formidable navies in the world, backing up with force the Roosevelt Corollary to the Monroe Doctrine, which established the nation's role as a "police power" in the Caribbean. From 1904 to 1914, U.S. naval power controlled the Atlantic and the Caribbean. At the advent of World War I, as the role of the U.S. Navy expanded, the need for coast artillery installations like Fort Screven diminished as foreign powers respected the Monroe Doctrine and the threat of attack became less likely.

Changes in the Twentieth Century

During the early years of World War I, while most of Europe was at war, the troops of the 14th Coast Artillery stationed at Fort Screven kept the post's guns prepared while coordinating land and sea patrols to guard against German U-boat incursions and other subversive activities. In 1917, Germany's declaration of unrestricted submarine warfare against all shipping in the Atlantic prompted the United States to reverse its position of neutrality and declare war on

Germany. Although German submarine activity increased along the east coast during this time, action along the South Carolina and Georgia coasts was minimal. As a result, in 1917–1918 Battery Brumby's four eight-inch guns and Battery Habersham's 12-inch rifled mortars were dismantled and sent to France for use in the war against Germany.

Following the end of World War I, coastal defense batteries like Fort Screven were considered obsolete and the coast artillery companies were withdrawn. As the U.S. Army was downsizing to peacetime levels, the War Department began the task of mothballing or closing surplus installations. In 1921 the department deactivated Fort Screven, leaving a small caretaker detachment of 2 officers and 30 troops to maintain the post. All but three of Fort Screven's big guns were dismantled and removed at this time.

In 1922 the War Department announced that Fort Screven would be reactivated as the Headquarters of the 8th Infantry Regiment, which arrived at the post in February 1923. The regiment had served with the occupation forces in Germany from 1919 to 1923 and was the last of the U.S. troops to leave Europe after World War I. Fort Screven entered into a second phase of construction during this time as the installation made the transition from coast artillery station to infantry post. Existing buildings were repaired and several new buildings, such as barracks and mess halls, were constructed to accommodate a greater number of troops.

One of the duties of the 8th Infantry included coordinating the Citizen's Military Training Program (CMTP), which established Citizens Military Training Camps (CMTC) under the 1920 National Defense Act. In fact, during the summer of 1921, before the War Department had decided what to do with the post, Fort Screven served as a training site for members of the CMTC from Georgia, South Carolina, and Florida, which included units of the 325th Infantry Reserve. After the 8th Infantry Regiment was assigned to the post, Fort Screven became a training command for the CMTP for Georgia and north Florida. Each summer, as part of their duties, soldiers of the 8th Infantry trained hundreds of CMTC troops one month and army reserve officers the following month. CMTC troops and army reserve officer trainees would be housed in tent camps in the open areas of the post near the battery. This army training program, which was conducted each summer at Fort Screven until 1941, was the forerunner of the Officer's Candidate School Program instituted at the beginning of World War II.

In 1929 the Headquarters of the 8th Infantry was moved to Fort Moultrie on Sullivan's Island near Charleston, leaving only one battalion, 1st Battalion, at

Fort Screven. During the 1930s Fort Screven continued its role as an important training command for the CMTP.

In the spring of 1932, Fort Screven came under the command of Lt. Colonel George Marshall, whose tour of duty on Tybee followed his position as assistant commandant at Fort Benning, the U.S. Army's infantry school near Columbus, Georgia. With a garrison of less than 400 men, Fort Screven was considered a small assignment, but Marshall welcomed the opportunity to assume his first military post command. During his tour at Fort Screven, Marshall concentrated his efforts on military training and the necessary housekeeping procedures for the post. Under Marshall the appearance of the post was improved through landscape additions and the careful maintenance of the grounds.

In 1933 President Franklin D. Roosevelt announced the establishment of the Civilian Conservation Corps (CCC), one of the first New Deal relief programs approved by Congress to help the nation get back on its feet during the Great Depression. The purpose of the CCC was to put thousands of unemployed young men to work in conservation projects that included reforestation, fighting forest fires, soil erosion control, and harnessing water power through the construction of dams. The U.S. Army was given the assignment of setting up and running the CCC camps, which involved the enrollment, organization, and administration of approximately 250,000 men across the nation. As a result of the army's involvement with the program, several CCC camps were set up on army posts and other federally owned property.

Lt. Colonel Marshall's greatest contribution while serving at Fort Screven was his enthusiastic involvement in establishing the CCC program in the region. With Fort Screven established as its headquarters, Marshall was named commanding officer of CCC District "F" of the IV Corp Area in 1933. Marshall and his staff were responsible for establishing, organizing, and supplying 19 CCC base camps throughout Georgia and Florida.

The first camp Marshall established was at Fort Screven. He used the CCC trainees assigned to Fort Screven to assist him in furthering his goals for the CMTP, another program he championed while at Fort Screven. One of the first projects assigned to the CCC workers at Fort Screven was the construction of temporary and permanent support buildings for the CMTC at the post. There were three distinct training areas established at Fort Screven for the CMTP. Training Area 1 was behind Battery Garland in the open space in front of the Tybee Light Station, Training Area 2 was in the open space south of the Tybee Light Station, and Training Area 3 was in the open space behind Batteries Backus and Gant. During the 1920s the three CMTC areas were little more than tent encampments set up in the undefined open space of the post. The work done by the CCC trainees established each of these open spaces into clearly defined training areas with permanent frame and concrete block support buildings that included an administration building, dispensary, mess halls, recreation halls, and latrines. The design for these training facilities clearly orients the fixed support buildings to the tent pads, which were arranged in military hierarchy by company and battalion.

Other CCC camps established nearby included one at Fort Pulaski and one at Hinesville, Georgia. Declared a national monument in 1924 by President Calvin Coolidge, Fort Pulaski was abandoned and in ruins when it was transferred to the National Park Service in 1933. The CCC workers assigned to Fort Pulaski provided the back breaking labor involved in restoring the masonry fort and developing the property for viewing by the public. Part of the work that the CCC trainees were involved in included the removal of the thick growth of brush and trees that had taken over the parade ground within the fort, the repair of masonry walls and buttressing, and the removal of years of mud and silt that had build up in the moat. One of the most formidable of the CCC projects conducted at Fort Pulaski included the construction of a bridge across the South Channel of the Savannah River in 1938 that connected Cockspur and McQueen Islands.

In the summer of 1933 Marshall was promoted to colonel and given the command of the 8th Infantry Regiment assigned to Fort Moultrie. After he had taken command of Fort Moultrie, Marshall received a special commendation from the inspector general's office "for his efficient and economical administration of his duties and the high morale of his command" while at Fort Screven. Marshall's abilities as a military leader were later recognized with his selection as U.S. Army chief of staff during World War II. After the war Marshall continued to serve his country as secretary of state, for which he is best known as the architect of the Marshall Plan for the economic recovery of western Europe. His efforts were later rewarded with the Nobel Peace Prize.

After 17 years at Fort Screven, the 1st Battalion, 8th Infantry Regiment was reassigned to Fort Benning, Georgia in June 1940. During the summer of 1940 the 2nd Battalion, 70th Coast Artillery garrisoned Fort Screven. The unit came to Fort Screven from Fort Monroe, Virginia with a compliment of 401 men and 107 vehicles. In September 1940 the 252nd Coast Artillery, North Carolina National Guard arrived at Fort Screven for training, bringing with them six of the unit's guns, which were transported to Savannah by train. For the next several months the National Guard troops of the 252nd were instructed by troops of the 70th stationed at Fort Screven. By the end of 1940 the 252nd Coast Artillery had returned to North Carolina and the 2nd Battalion, 70th Coast Artillery was reassigned to the newly established Camp Stewart at Hinesville, Georgia. The departure of the 70th marked the end of Fort Screven's use as an infantry post.

During World War II, Fort Screven became a training command center for the U.S. Corps of Engineers Deep Sea Diving and Salvage School, the U.S. Army's only training facility for beginning divers. Fort Screven served as an administration center while actual hands-on instruction was conducted at a training camp established near Chimney Creek on the west side of the island. From 1941 to 1943 engineer units were organized into port construction and repair groups and trained to clear ports in Africa and Europe of sunken ships and ordnance in anticipation of an impending allied invasion.

Engineer units trained at Fort Screven during this time included the 1051st, 1052nd, 1053rd, and 1054th Engineer Port Construction and Repair Groups. Most members of these units brought prior experience and skills from their civilian occupations that made them particularly useful for this service. Unit members included engineers, divers, mechanics, welders, and others. Applicants had to pass strict physical tests and were subjected to 12 intensive weeks of training. As part of their training, engineer units worked on various construction projects for the post and the local community. These included the construction of a new post exchange restaurant in 1943, a bridge and part of a highway at Camp Stewart in Hinesville, and a municipal dock for the city of Savannah Beach on Tybee. Fort Screven continued to serve in this capacity until the army no longer had a need for additional trained divers and salvage crews.

In 1944 the War Department announced that Fort Screven was one of several installations across the nation that had been declared surplus since they were left empty when most of the enlisted men had been transferred overseas. Fort Screven was deactivated in October 1944, and in 1945 the land and buildings that made up the post were dispensed to the city of Savannah Beach through the Federal Housing Authority. Savannah Beach purchased the property from the federal government for $230,000 and, in January of 1946, offered the entire Fort Screven property, which included approximately 135 acres and 265 buildings, for sale. The sole bid was made by the Robinson Realty Company on behalf of the Fort Screven Development Company. Property exempt from the sale included the five acre Tybee Island Lighthouse and Coast Guard station, which was retained by the federal government, and several maintenance and service-related buildings that were seen as useful to the city. Buildings retained by the city for municipal use included the fire station, gymnasium, telephone exchange, post exchange, sewer and water pumps, crane building and shop, automobile workshop, and garage. Following the successful bid for the property, the Fort Screven Development Company separated the post into individual lots and offered the various buildings for sale. By the 1950s many of Fort Screven's buildings had been converted for use as year-round residences, seasonal rentals, apartments, and summer houses.

Chapter Four

BUILDING A COASTAL RESORT

Interest in Tybee as a place for recreation began as early as the mid nineteenth century. Beginning in the 1840s, pleasure excursions to Tybee were offered in which steamers carried excursionists to the island to spend the day. Advertisements in the Savannah papers stressed the health-giving air and refreshing breezes of the island. A news article in the July 4, 1851 issue of the *Daily Morning News* gave the following account of one such excursion:

> On Wednesday morning, the steamer, J. Stone, with a large party went on a pleasure excursion to Fort Pulaski and Tybee. The party landed at the Fort, and were conducted through the building. After the party returned to the boat a sumptuous collation was spread. In the afternoon the boat proceeded to Tybee where a large number of gentlemen embraced the opportunity to take a sea bath.

As a result of these trips, the beginnings of a resort were starting to take shape on the island. Old maps of Tybee indicate that a hostelry of some kind, called Hotel Bolton, was established near the lighthouse as early as the late 1850s. The hotel was undoubtedly built in response to increasing interest in Tybee. The outbreak of the Civil War, however, ended steamer excursions to the island, thereby ending any possibility of additional development on Tybee until after the war.

Steamer excursions to the island resumed immediately following the end of the Civil War, and by the late 1860s, day trips to Tybee had become a very popular source of recreation. Realizing the island's untapped potential, a group of Savannah entrepreneurs formed the Tybee Improvement Company for the purpose of promoting the development of Tybee as a seaside resort. In 1873, the company obtained possession of the island, established a regularly scheduled steamer route, and began developing a plan for the subdivision of the island into building lots. To encourage lot sales, plans were also made for the construction of a hotel on the South End of the island. A wooden tramway was deemed the best way to transport guests from the steamship pier on the North End to the resort along the oceanfront. As an added amenity, plans were made to extend the horse railway the length of Main Street (later Butler Avenue) to the Inlet in order to provide guests with the option of bathing in the calm waters of the Back River.

An article in the September 11, 1874 issue of the *Savannah Morning News* announced the completion of the survey of Tybee and described the lots that were being made available:

> The project of converting Tybee Island into a summer resort has been the topic of discussion in this community for the past two years, but until lately nothing really definite has been done toward accomplishing this very desirable end. Now, however, there is a fair prospect that when the "dog star" for 1875 commences such arrangements will have been completed which will at least enable our people to make frequent daily trips to this charming spot and enjoy the luxury of a surf bath and other sources of pleasure while abroad. A survey of the island, exclusive of the northern portions, which was lately sold to the government, shows we believe 300 good sized lots, sufficiently large to give every building erected thereon a fine garden. The lots we understand will be assessed at $200.00.

The survey, entitled "Plan of a Part of Tybee Island," by John Tebeau, indicates that many of the lots along the oceanfront and the Savannah River had already been sold before the plan had been printed. Most of the lots sold along the oceanfront were in close proximity to the site of the hotel that the stockholders were planning to build. The construction of a hotel to encourage development was already beginning to show results.

In 1876, the hotel, named the Ocean House, as well as the horse railway, was completed. On March 24 the following year, the *Savannah Morning News* described an excursion to the new resort during what must have been the beginning of its first season:

> Yesterday afternoon the fine steamer Cumberland made the excursion to Tybee Island with the Directors of the Tybee Improvement Company. . . . The run to the wharf was made against the wind and tide in one hour and thirty minutes. . . . On arriving at the island the party . . . was transported over the tramway to the south end. Here an hour was pleasantly passed strolling along the beach, and rambling through the hotel, en passant, is a most conveniently constructed and neatly finished building. The rooms are all plastered, of good size and well ventilated. A magnificent double piazza, front and back, affords a most delightful promenade . . . whilst the large

and commodious dinning room can at short notice be transformed into a splendid ballroom.

Additional accounts of the hotel further describe it as a three story structure having the dimensions 112 by 40 feet, with 40 sleeping rooms, a parlor, and a reception room.

From the very beginning of the resort, an effort was made through advertisements to convince Savannahians to spend their summers (and money) at home rather than travel north to the resorts from which Tybee's character was fashioned. The *Savannah Morning News* was an enthusiastic proponent of the venture, as one of its editors was also a company stockholder. As Cynthia Miller points out in "Tybee Island, Georgia: Changing Images and Land Uses, 1733–1895," the paper served as the primary image maker for the Tybee Improvement Company through its detailed editorials and articles extolling the virtues of the resort, which were always found to be superior to those of the northern resorts. The paper's articles "compared the quality of the beach, waves, hotels, services, and even patrons," and never found Tybee lacking in any category. The accounts skillfully played on the sensitivities of Savannahians. As Miller said of this *c.* 1877 piece, "perhaps the most explicit of these articles bluntly reminded Georgians of one of [their] most sacred possessions—their Southern heritage:"

> It seems a strange oversight or neglect that Savannah has gone so long with no seaside resort. . . . Hitherto it has been a necessity for those desiring to renew health or seek pleasure, to travel among strangers, to be cooped in a little dog hole; to be snobbed by shoddy aristocrats; to have wife, sister, or daughter hob nobbing with the cher ami of some Yankee parvenue, for it is a well known fact that among the swell mob at all Yankee watering places there is a strange sprinkling of couples who are married only by brevet, and it is impossible for strangers to tell the chaff from the wheat. Now however, all for the mere passage north, anyone may spend the month by the murmuring sea in a large and airy room, surrounded by friends and within an hours reach of home and physician.
>
> Let us see, now people of Savannah, which you will chose, and what manner of men ye be.

Savannah's Popular Resort

The resort was such a success that by the early 1880s, the steamer routes were running at full capacity. The stockholders realized that they had to increase passenger volume to the island if they were going to develop on a larger scale. It was agreed by all concerned that a railroad to the island would solve this problem. However, constructing the line across 15 miles of marsh was considered impossible at the time. As a result, few investors would take a risk on the venture and the project was abandoned.

Unable to take the resort to the next level, the Tybee Improvement Company sold a controlling interest in the island to Captain Daniel G. Purse in 1885. Captain Purse, a Savannah entrepreneur, designed an embankment that could sustain the weight of a train traveling through the marsh. After soliciting financial backing from his peers (many of whom had been stockholders in the now defunct Tybee Improvement Company), the project was put back in motion. In 1887 the Savannah and Tybee Railroad was completed. The train not only cut traveling time to Tybee in half, it also made the entire island more accessible by offering eight stops between the North End and the Inlet (South End). By the early 1900s each stop had been named (in order of arrival): Estill Station, Fort Screven Station, Lovell Station, Atlantic Club Station, 11th Street Station, Dixon Station, Tybee Station (at the resort center), and Inlet Station (where the turnstile was located on the Back River).

The Tybee Beach Company was formed earlier in 1887 to supervise and control the further development of the island. The completion of the railroad brought on a burst of new development that was concentrated around the Ocean House. The increase in lot sales resulted in the building of more summer cottages. By the end of 1887, Tybee was incorporated by the general assembly of Georgia as the Town of Ocean City. One year later the name was changed to the Town of Tybee. A September 6, 1888 *Savannah Morning News* article entitled "Tybee Island, Savannah's Popular Summer Resort," described the overwhelming success the resort was enjoying in the late 1880s:

> The number of visitors these last four months is estimated at eighty thousand. . . . A continuous stream of visitors from the city as well as the interior poured into Tybee, far exceeding the capacity of the hotels and boarding houses to entertain them. Excursions, particularly from Augusta, were very frequent, and all pronounced the beach-surf bathing equal to any from Narragansett Bay to the capes of Florida. It is understood that several parties in the latter city invested in Tybee lots, with the view of erecting sea side cottages for the occupation of their families during the summer. . . . Since the last season, considerable improvements have been made on the island, and the

accommodations more than doubled. Besides the Ocean House, we now have Furber's Point House, Mrs. Lee's Seaside Pavilion, and the Ocean View Hotel.

Each of the boarding houses and hotels at the resort had its own dancing pavilions and bathhouses. The summer cottages that were built during that time each had private, one-room bathhouses on the beach.

Once the resort proved popular with Savannahians, the stockholders began a campaign to attract more guests from outside the city. With the construction of more hotels and boarding houses, and with the availability of lots for summer cottages, the resort could accommodate more people than ever before. With a good infrastructure in place, including a first class transportation system, the island had great potential. In an effort to lure southerners away from northern resorts, the stockholders began to run advertisements that directly compared the resort on Tybee with its northern competitors. Like the earlier ads in the *Savannah Morning News*, Tybee was always found to be equal or superior to any of the northern resorts. B. H. Richardson's "A History of Tybee Island, Ga., and a Sketch of the Savannah and Tybee Railroad," in which Tybee is referred to as the "Long Branch of the South," is an excellent example of the type of articles and advertisements written at that time to promote the resort:

> New York has her Long Branch, New Jersey her Cape May, Maryland her Eastern Shore, Rhode Island her Nantuckett, and Savannah, equally fortunate, scarcely realized that she had at her arms length, as it were, an Island with attractions and resources capable of development that would compare favorably as a pleasure resort with any of the places named. . . . this beach presents a scene of rare attractiveness and beauty, rivaling in a measure the panoramas of life and beauty which renders Long Branch, New Port, Cape May, and Nantuckett renowned; and in the near future, when fully fruition crowns the plan already inaugurated and in process of execution, Tybee will rank among the most noted of the pleasure resorts of the country.

Hotel Tybee

In 1888, The Tybee Beach Company announced plans for the construction of a first class hotel near the southernmost end of the island. On September 6, 1888 the *Savannah Morning News* reported the stockholders plans for the construction of a "mammoth hotel:"

The premises and grounds will embrace 20 acres, and it is the determination of the company to make the building and its appurtenances first class in every respect; elevators, water, electric lights and all the modern improvements and appliances will be provided. In short, it is intended to make the hotel a popular resort for invalids and tourists during the winter months where they may breath the invigorating atmosphere and enjoy warm cold [*sic*] salt baths and the pleasures of sailing, hunting, and fishing at will.

A civil engineer was hired that same year to plot off the rest of the island in anticipation of the increase in lot sales, particularly on the South End, that would follow the announcement of the new hotel. When the plan was completed in 1890, all the lots on the Inlet had already been sold.

In 1891 Hotel Tybee was completed for a sum of $80,000. Built facing the ocean "in plain view of the breakers rolling in from the Atlantic," the new hotel was an impressive, three story, Queen Anne style building with pedimented gable roof dormers, three-sided bay windows, fluted square columns, round archways, and an extensive one story piazza that extended the entire length of the south elevation and façade of the building. The hotel was equipped with its own artesian waterworks and featured a large, lavishly appointed dining room, parlor, and a covered, five-story observation platform on the roof of the building. Other amenities included separate dancing and picnic pavilions, saloon, and bath house building. With over 100 rooms, the new hotel had nearly triple the capacity of the Ocean House.

With the completion of Hotel Tybee, the island had truly entered into the same class as the northern resorts. Lots were sold and summer cottages were built along the oceanfront between Hotel Tybee and the Ocean House. The South End of the island started to be developed. A few summer cottages were built along the inlet, and a sparse collection of dancing pavilions, bath houses, boarding houses, and other service oriented businesses began to develop around the new hotel. By the mid 1890s, horse racing, concerts, dancing, and vaudeville shows were among the activities that were available to resort patrons. Also during this time, several private clubs were established on Tybee, including the Chatham Artillery Club (*c.*1888) and the Tybee Inlet Club (*c.* 1895) along the Inlet, or Back River, on Tybee's South End, and the Atlantic Club and Zorida Archery Club (*c.* 1885) along the ocean side of Main Street, on the corners of 8th and 10th Streets, respectively. Each of these clubs maintained large buildings and grounds offering members all the amenities of a small hotel.

The Central of Georgia: "The Right Way"

Tybee became a regional resort when the railroad became a unit of the Central of Georgia in 1890, followed by its direct ownership in 1895. This new affiliation gave the island a direct link to hundreds of towns and cities throughout Georgia and Alabama. The vast transportation network of the Central of Georgia had a tremendous effect on Tybee, as described in an early twentieth century promotional brochure:

> Approximately a quarter of a million passengers, hailing from many states in the Union, are handled every year to Tybee by the Central of Georgia Railway. Low rate excursion fares from points in Georgia, Alabama, and other southeastern states during the season help to make the annual Tybee trip comparatively inexpensive. To reach Tybee, persons in Georgia and Alabama will find their most comfortable trip via Central of Georgia to Savannah, thence via the Central's Tybee Branch to the beach. From points outside these two states, it is advisable to travel via Atlanta, Birmingham, Montgomery, Augusta, Athens, Americus, Albany, or any other principal gateway, thence via the lines of the Central—THE RIGHT WAY.

The Central of Georgia was a key factor in Tybee's development as a major seaside resort. Not only did the railroad provide the transportation network to bring tourists from the interior of Georgia and the South, the company was also an avid promoter of Tybee through its regional marketing and advertising campaigns. Each year the Central published a promotional brochure highlighting destinations and sights that could be visited along its railway system in an effort to entice people to travel via their network. Tybee, which was a very popular summer destination, proved to be a very profitable line for the company. Tybee was always included prominently in the company's literature, as evidenced in the 1897 brochure *Southern Scenes . . . Points and Pictures along the Central of Georgia Railway*:

> From May first to September the finest surf bathing along the Southern Atlantic coast is enjoyed at this popular seashore resort. The people of Savannah, eighteen miles away, together with hundreds who take advantage of the cheap excursion rates offered via the Central of Georgia Railway from interior Georgia, Alabama and other Southern points, daily visit Tybee and are refreshed and invigorated from the summer sun by the salt surf baths and the cool ocean breezes. The beach during the bathing hours presents a lively appearance. Bright

bathing costumes, laughing and playing children, gaily attired men and women offer to the eye a pleasing picture. This beach is of pure white sand, with a gradual slope of 100 feet or more into the ocean. The various hostelries at Tybee have all the modern conveniences and ample accommodations. This is Georgia's greatest seaside resort. Connected with Savannah by a perfect train service of the Central of Georgia Railway.

A Cyclone of Death

Although the resorts on Tybee prospered and grew during the 1890s, the Tybee Beach Company found there was one factor they could not control or predict: the weather. Devastating hurricanes in 1893, 1896, and again in 1898 caused hundreds of thousands of dollars in damage, destroying several dozen cottages, pavilions, bath houses, wood walkways, and platforms, and all the other various amenities and equipment of a coastal resort.

Of these hurricanes, the 1893 storm was the most devastating and as such, the most widely recalled. The hurricane, which weather historians now believe was a Category 3 storm with winds of 110 miles per hour or more, created a swath of destruction from the Florida border to North Carolina. Hundreds of houses were unroofed or swept away altogether and scores of vessels were left wrecked on the coast. The barrier islands were particularly hard hit as related through grisly newspaper accounts such as this from the *Savannah Morning News*: "On the sea islands, swept by the full fury of the storm, negroes were drowned by the hundreds. Day after day the receding waters gave up their ghastly harvest of the dead. As in war, long trenches were dug to receive the bodies."

Newspapers gave other accounts of whole families wiped out and of the pestilence spread by hundreds of unburied corpses left along the coast and low lying areas. According to the National Weather Service, the hurricane, which killed over 2,000 people in Georgia and South Carolina, was one of the five deadliest hurricanes in U.S. history. The *Savannah Morning News* published an account of the storm two days later under a sensational headline that gave a summary of the devastation: "A Cyclone of Death. Fifteen Bodies Recovered So Far. Twice That Number of People Missing. A Score of Vessels Wrecked. Tybee Almost Wiped Out. The Damage to Property Beyond Estimate."

On the day the hurricane made landfall on Tybee, Sunday August 27, 1893, most of the summer residents had evacuated the island, having left on a special train that was sent before communications were cut off. That night Tybee was pounded by the hurricane for 10 hours, with winds in excess of 90 miles per hour and flood waters rising 19 feet above sea level.

The devastation wrought by the storm was recalled in great detail in a letter written by Margaret Workman to her uncle only one week after the ordeal. Workman and her family, having abandoned their own cottage in the vicinity of the Ocean House, rode out the storm with other families at the Blun House, "just this side of the new hotel [Hotel Tybee], almost a mile and a quarter."

From Workman's letter it is apparent that apart from Hotel Tybee, the hurricane left few buildings standing on the island:

> The next morning broke clear and bright, though windy, and we all went down to the cottages to see what damage had been done, the water having almost receded. What demolition met us on every side— articles of every description, remnants of chairs, mattresses, baskets, trunks, pieces of furniture, everything in fact, and the beach from the railroad track down to the ocean as clean a sweep as the regular beach at low tide, not a sand dune to be seen.

Although the hotel survived the storm, the railroad was completely destroyed, with the track "torn up and twisted, some being a quarter of a mile away, standing on end like a fence—even the rail bed is gone." As described in Workman's letter, the devastation to the resort, particularly the area surrounding the Ocean House, appears to have been total:

> But for the Naylor House down there is hardly a house left . . . ships turned bottom up on one side of us, and on the land side house [*sic*] all splintered, not even seeing the pillars upon which they rested.

The railroad was rebuilt in time for the 1894 season, although the appearance of the resort had been changed dramatically as several staple hostelries had apparently been destroyed. The Ocean House, Furber's Point House, the Ocean View Hotel—all part of the original resort area concentrated near Lovell Station—are not present on the Sanborn Fire Insurance Map of 1898. Reports indicating that the Lovell Station area was particularly hard hit support the assumption that these buildings were destroyed during the 1893 hurricane, or perhaps the subsequent hurricane of 1896.

Development of the Oceanfront Resort Center

With the loss of the Ocean House, Hotel Tybee on the South End of the island had become the new center of the resort by 1900. As a result, the construction of a second large hotel, called the South End Hotel, was completed along 16th Street one block south of Hotel Tybee during the late 1890s. The South End

Hotel was a large two story frame building with an attached one story pavilion, dining room, and bar. The hostelry also featured a row of one story frame duplex rental cottages as an alternative for hotel patrons.

In an effort to entice people to come to the resort by way of their rail system, The Central of Georgia built an enormous dancing and entertainment pavilion, the Tybrisa, next to Hotel Tybee about 1900. The Tybrisa, which was located in front of the South End Hotel Complex on the corner of 16th Street and Strand, was Tybee's largest and most well known pavilion. The Tybrisa pavilion was a large, one story, hip roof structure raised on wood piers that extended out over the beach beyond the high water mark. The dance floor and bandstand was located in the center of the pavilion, while rocking chairs lined the wraparound verandah on its outer edges. The Tybrisa complex also featured men's and women's bath houses, which were raised on piers parallel to the pavilion. A one story dining room, bar, and café was located behind the pavilion along 16th Street. Wood walkways and platforms connected all the buildings that made up the Tybrisa. Along with Hotel Tybee, the Tybrisa was the heart of the resort during the early 1900s.

In 1908 Hotel Tybee was destroyed by fire. In 1911 it was replaced by a new three-and-a-half story, 150-room concrete building constructed on the same site. The new Hotel Tybee was the finest hostelry ever built on the island. Advertisements proclaimed it "One of the Finest Resort Hotels on the Atlantic Coast between Atlantic City and Palm Beach." The scale and quality of the new complex reflected Tybee's growing stature as the south Atlantic's premier coastal resort. The new Hotel Tybee building reflected the latest trends at other major resorts, particularly those in Florida, which was enjoying a boom period of resort construction and development. During this time, seaside resort hotels in Florida were built to reflect the Spanish origins of the state, which became a trademark of Florida tourism used in enticing wealthy northerners south to the Sunshine State. The resort hotels constructed in Florida at this time were built with a permanence and elegance not commonly found at southern resorts, which were usually frame with clapboard siding and wide wraparound verandahs—in other words, the buildings resembled oversized boarding houses. The construction of such an elegant building on Tybee was meant to lend the resort an exotic appeal and sophistication that would set it apart from other southern resorts while touting Georgia's own Spanish origins.

The new Hotel Tybee, which actually displayed a combination of both the Italian Renaissance and Spanish Colonial Revival styles, was built facing the ocean and featured a main, three-and-a-half story hip mass with two story wings that projected out from the corners of the building on the ocean side, creating a half-formed U-shape. The formal façade of the building, which faced Main Street, was balanced by two square, five story observation towers at each end of the main section. The roof was covered with red tiles and featured widely overhanging eaves with large decorative paired cornice-line brackets. The building was finished with a smooth stucco exterior and featured a one story, pergola-like verandah along the side of the building facing the ocean.

The new hotel was received with great fanfare when it formally opened for the 1911 season on June 1 of that year. The opening was celebrated with a gala dinner reception that evening with over 250 guests and dignitaries from Savannah in attendance. Hotel Tybee was seen as the crown jewel of the resort, as described in this glowing description of the building and grounds in the *Savannah Morning News*:

> Equipped with everything possible which makes for the comfort and pleasure of its guests the Hotel Tybee is one of the finest seashore hotels on the Eastern coast. It is situated about a half mile from the south end of the island and is set back from the strand about one hundred yards. The hotel is so situated as to afford the quiet for those who wish to rest and still is near enough to the center of social activity for all those who wish to engage in that sort of life. There is a long pier covered for the most part extending from the entrance of the hotel to the pavilion and bath houses operated by the hotel management. On this covered pier there are large numbers of covered porch rockers in which one may sit and enjoy the cool, fresh breezes from the sea while the distant roll of the breakers on the strand lends a romantic air to the scene. Picturesque in its setting among the sand dunes and wild grasses Hotel Tybee is of Spanish architectural design and finished in tinted stucco and red tile roof and is so constructed that most of the rooms have the advantage of the sea breeze. It was constructed but a few years ago and is of fireproof construction throughout. There is a large dining room which looks out onto the ocean in the distance and several private dining rooms including one on the verandah. The grounds of the hotel is planted with many colored flowers and no effort is spared to make for the perfect comfort of its guests. The cuisine is excellent, a specialty being made of the seafoods peculiar to this section. . . . There is an up-to-date barber shop and soda fountain in the building. This hotel contains a spacious lobby furnished with numbers of comfortable chairs and has many tastefully decorated parlors and rest rooms. Besides there are writing rooms arranged in such a way that every comfort may be enjoyed while one is doing his corresponding.

In addition to the accommodations of the main building, Hotel Tybee also offered resort patrons the option of staying in one of its four-room cottages, which were situated in a row along 15th Street. The cottages, which were part of the original Hotel Tybee complex, were built *c.* 1900 and were a highlighted amenity in the hotel's literature:

> A feature of the hotel is it's cottages. These are twelve in number. Few hotels have such accommodations where families and parties may be served with as much privacy as if they were in their own home. Every convenience has been given to these cottages. . . . This cottage feature is brought to the highest perfection at Hotel Tybee.

A covered walkway connected the hotel to the pavilion, which was located on the beach at the end of 15th Street near the high tide mark. The Hotel Tybee Pavilion was a large, two story front gabled structure raised on wood piers. The bath house was situated on the ground floor and the dancing pavilion was located on the top floor, which was fully open. During the season, the hotel would sponsor dances several nights of the week in which a good orchestra would provide live music. Adjacent to the bath house/pavilion was a one story refreshment pavilion, which, during the 1910s, was called Levan's Café. The long, bleacher-like steps that lead from the boardwalk in front of the pavilion down to the beach was a favorite place for large gatherings of people to stage group photos during the 1910s and 1920s.

In addition to the main hotel building, the row of hotel cottages, and the hotel pavilion, the complex also included a manager's cottage, a separate servants' cottage and dining room, and a pool room (located in a separate building behind the pavilion). Occupying a full city block between 14th and 15th Streets, and extending from Butler Avenue to the beach, the buildings that made up the complex were arranged in an informal, yet picturesque landscape complete with a lush expanse of grass that extended from the ocean side of the hotel down to the strand, planted flower beds, palmettos, and palm tree–lined paths and walkways.

The principal attractions of the resort on Tybee's South End were firmly established with the construction of Bohan's Pavilion at the end of 15th Street during the late 1900s. Located along the strand between Hotel Tybee and the Tybrisa complex, the establishment featured two large bath houses, one for men and one for women, a dancing pavilion and restaurant, and an assortment of refreshment stands. Its proximity to Hotel Tybee made it popular with non-guests who had come to spend the day at the beach but did not have the use of the hotel's amenities. By the mid 1910s the establishment became Durden and Powers Pavilion.

Where Ocean Breezes Blow

During the early years of the resort, the summer season on Tybee generally began on May 1 and ended September 1. Many of the hotels, such as Hotel Tybee, which was open from May 15 through September 1, would close down during the winter months. Maintenance, additions, and improvements to the resort infrastructure would take place during the winter in preparation for the coming season. Advertisements in the local paper during the early weeks of May would herald the approach of the new resort season, always promising new and improved attractions and amenities. The 1916 season was no different. A full page ad was taken out in the Saturday, May 27 edition of the *Savannah Morning News* that featured dozens of advertisements for the resort's various businesses, all under a decorative heading that read "TYBEE—Where Ocean Breezes Blow."

The Central of Georgia's advertisement announcing the commencement of summer service to the island echoed a blanket theme of renewal and improvement for the entire resort:

> A NEW AND BEAUTIFIED TYBEE awaits your inspection. There is the same old broad Atlantic, the same cooling breezes that have for decades breathed romance and health and comfort, but there are radical improvements, new attractions, glad surprises, remodeled buildings. It's the same old TYBEE but in her summer finery. You will want to call it "spotless town." The best amusement features obtainable have been secured and there are "things happening" every minute.

The Tybee Pavilion Company, which had recently leased and taken over the operation of the Tybrisa from the Central of Georgia Railroad, ran an advertisement announcing the completion of a $10,000 renovation of the whole pavilion, leaving the structure "clean, orderly, and inviting." With a caption that read "THE NEW TYBEE PAVILION," the Tybee Pavilion Company's advertisement promised a seaside paradise for its patrons during the 1916 season:

> It is no trouble to be comfortable when all that one desires is within easy reach and to be had for the asking. This is one of the reasons why the new Tybee Pavilion is destined to be the Mecca for the people who visit Tybee during the season. Here is music, here is cuisine of the highest

quality, here are the people you like to meet, the dancing, the better class of amusements, the great cool, inviting promenade overlooking the rolling surf, cooling beverages for the thirsty, easy chairs in which to lounge away the spare hours. All of these prerequisites, have been carefully planned for by the Tybee Pavilion Management, in order to meet the tastes of the whole people, and yet be accessible at only a nominal cost. The A-La-Carte restaurant, together with the quick order lunch counter, are under supervision of the South's finest caters and can supply anything from a light lunch to a course dinner, with the best service obtainable. Dancing on the great area, is indulged in every afternoon and until 10 p.m. . . . and on Saturdays until 11:15 p.m. Automatic baseball and a shooting gallery are in operation and a soda fountain dispenses ice cream at the small tables at all hours. The best cigars and tobaccos are sold. There is an excellent children's playground under the pavilion.

While the Hotel Tybee Pavilion was popular with guests of the hotel and the Durden and Powers Pavilion catered to patrons of the small hotels and boarding houses, the Tybrisa Pavilion was especially popular with the masses of day trippers who arrived on the island on the first train to spend the day at the seashore. The Tybrisa was less expensive than the other pavilions, which made it attractive to working and middle class families who might not have the means for overnight accommodations but would nevertheless like to "take in the salts." In advertisements the Tybrisa was billed as "Tybee's pavilion" and as the "very heart of the resort" in an effort to appeal to this niche market. Daytrippers were implored to come to the Tybrisa, where all their needs could be met in one place:

> Whether your desire is to take sea baths, dance to inspiring music, eat a good dinner, see all the best attractions, recline in restful repose in an easy chair, or seek the society of your friends, the one place where you can do any one or all these things, is on the Tybee Pavilion. . . . You don't have to go anywhere else to look for anything. The Tybee Pavilion Management is prepared for your summer entertainment. Come direct to us from the train, make our pavilion your headquarters while on the island.

By the end of the 1910s, thousands had done just that—gone directly from the train and down the walkway from Main Street to the strand, where a wooden platform between the Tybrisa Bathhouses and the Tybrisa Pavilion provided access directly into the ocean. Because Tybrisa was so popular, this boardwalk was dubbed "the entrance to the ocean," with the walkway later being named Atlantic Avenue. Tybee Station, the train stop for patrons coming to the resort, even had a sign over the station that said "Main entrance to the Ocean." Atlantic Avenue became the unofficial "main street" leading to the resort. As a result, numerous vendors set up soda and hotdog stands, bait shops, ice cream stands, cigar shops, amusement and novelty stands, and other small businesses along the corridor. A wooden boardwalk connected Tybrisa with the Durden and Powers and Hotel Tybee Pavilions, unifying the oceanfront resort area along the strand.

As a result of the overwhelming success of the resort, a number of small hotels, boarding houses, restaurants, and other service-oriented businesses had been established around and in the vicinity of the resort area by 1920. The 150-room Sea Breeze Hotel, which replaced the South End Hotel on Atlantic Avenue during the 1910s, and the Ocean View Hotel (*c.* 1910), located on the corner of 16th and Main Streets, offered a less pretentious alternative to Hotel Tybee while still allowing patrons close proximity to the dancing pavilions and other attractions of the resort. In addition to these smaller hostels, a number of boarding houses had been established near the strand along Izlar Avenue, south of 16th Street and the resort area. The corridor was named after E. B. Izlar, who operated a row of eight boarding houses situated on both sides of the street, which was really little more than a lane. The Inlet Hotel, formerly the Tybee Inlet Club (*c.* 1890s), and Bynum's Riverside House (*c.* 1900), both located along Chatham Avenue, offered accommodations to those preferring the relative calm of the Inlet, or Back River, to the frenetic bustle of the resort. In addition to the small hotels and boarding houses, many of which offered weekly, monthly, and even seasonal rates, there were several cottages available for rent. A "house party group" would often rent part of or a whole cottage during a weekend or holiday period. The Smith Cottages on 17th Street and the Stults Cottages on Chatham Avenue (along the Back River) were particularly popular during this time.

A Year-Round Community

By the 1910s Tybee had begun to develop a small year-round population and, as a result, small villages developed near the resort and around Estill Station, near Fort Screven. The only grocery stores on the island during this time were established in these communities. Naylor's Store near Fort Screven, which catered to the soldiers during the off season; and S. F. Smith's store, near the resort, along the railroad track at the corner of Inlet Avenue and Main Street.

Smith's Grocery catered to the seasonal residents who "summered" on Tybee every year at private cottage developments that had been established along the strand (north of the resort along the ocean between 14th and 12th Streets) and along the Back River near the Inlet (Colony Row), as well as those renting cottages near the resort for an extended stay.

Other community buildings established by this time included a town hall, the Tybee Island School, and St. Michael's Church, all located along Main Street in the vicinity of Lovell Station.

The Tybee School was built in 1901 and was a frame, one-and-a-half story building with clapboard exterior and gable roof dormers along the sides of the roof. The building was raised on a wood pier foundation, which was common for buildings on Tybee during the late nineteenth and early twentieth century. The first floor contained a one room classroom while the second floor served as a loft apartment for the school teacher.

St. Michaels Catholic Church was the first church established on the island. Built in 1891, the building was a modest, one room clapboard church with a hint of Carpenter Gothic embellishment. The church was built on the corner of Main and Eighth Streets, opposite the Atlantic Club. The lot was donated by the Tybee Beach Company at the insistence of Captain Purse, chairman of the Tybee Beach Company, and Robert E. Pepper, president of the Atlantic Club. According to local accounts, the number of Catholic residents on Tybee was large enough to warrant the construction of a year-round chapel. During the resort season, the church was attended by tourists and members of the Atlantic Club, who were largely a Catholic community. The Diocese of Savannah sent a priest each weekend to hear confession on Saturday and to say Mass on Sunday morning. Until a rectory was built during the 1920s, the visiting priest would stay overnight in the "sleeping room" located on one side of the altar.

Although the resort on Tybee had achieved an unprecedented level of success during the 1910s, Tybee officials were already contemplating the best way to bring the development of the island to an even higher plateau. In an effort to keep the momentum of the resort going and to ensure that Tybee remained up to date with its competitors, officials from the town of Tybee, the city of Savannah, and Chatham County began discussing the feasibility of building an automobile road to link Tybee and Savannah as early as 1915. As with the completion of the Savannah-Tybee Railroad nearly 40 years earlier, the completion of the Tybee Road in 1923 would forever change the face of the Island.

Chapter Five

WHERE THE GEORGIA PEACHES GO

The level of success enjoyed by the resorts on Tybee during the late nineteenth and early twentieth centuries, as well as the growth of the town of Tybee as a year-round community during the 1900s and 1910s, was made entirely possible by the direct accessibility afforded the island by reliable, daily train service. Although other seaside resorts were established in Georgia as well as in other southern states, Tybee was the only resort on the south Atlantic coast outside Florida in which rail service carried passengers practically to the doorstep of their resort destination. While other resorts, like St. Simons Island, Georgia, still relied on steamers well into the twentieth century to transport resort patrons from the mainland to their isolated and otherwise inaccessible resorts, direct rail service to Tybee had been offered for almost 40 years. Rail service not only made the resort more accessible to those coming to vacation during the summer season, it made it easier and less expensive to transport building materials, making new construction on the island more affordable, and therefore facilitating the construction of summer cottages, boarding houses, etc. on the island. Reliable, daily rail service also made year-round living on Tybee more feasible. By 1920, Tybee was one of the most developed barrier islands on the south Atlantic coast.

A Modern Sea-shore City

In the same way that the train had replaced the steamer as Tybee's chief transportation system in the late nineteenth century, by the mid 1910s steps were being taken to construct an automobile road between Savannah and Tybee Island. The introduction in 1908 of Henry Ford's inexpensive and highly reliable Model-T made the automobile available to most middle-class Americans for the first time. The construction of the eastern section of the Dixie Highway between Michigan and Miami during the late 1910s provided greater travel opportunities for motorists and their families, stimulating auto-related commerce along the route as a result of a burgeoning new industry— auto tourism. With thousands traveling to Florida each year, the town of Tybee, as well as Chatham County, saw the wisdom in ensuring that Tybee became a destination along the new Dixie Highway, or at least a stop along the way. Elected officials on Tybee and in Savannah saw the benefits inherent in connecting the city and the resort, while the Chatham County board of commissioners, who would play a key role in making the Tybee Road possible, saw the opportunities for growth that the road would bring to the undeveloped sections of the county lying along the road's path. Judge Bacon, chairman of the board of commissioners, while speaking at a Rotary Club meeting on the eve of the opening of the Tybee Road, enumerated the reasons why the road was in the best interests of all involved:

> What physical developments can reasonably be expected to result from the construction of this road? You can expect to see colonies established and the rich lands so long idle on Oatland and Whitmarsh Islands developed into fruit and truck farms. You can expect to see a beautiful settlement on Turner's Rock or Lacey's Island. . . . Already a subdivision has been made and an attractive sign to the entrance of the property from Victory Drive invites prospective property owners to drive in over a paved road recently built and select their building lots. You can expect to see a modern tourist hotel with all that goes with it. Pavilions and summer homes erected on Wilmington Island. You can expect to see Tybee Island come into its own and become in reality a modern sea-shore city and the playground of Georgia.

Working together, the Tybee Road was built by the three governments with each constructing the section of road lying within their jurisdiction. In 1921 the city of Savannah built three-tenths mile of road from Waters Avenue to the city limits. That same year Chatham County built two miles of asphalt road from the Savannah city limits to the village of Thunderbolt on the Wilmington River. Work on the main portion of the Tybee Road, in which 14.3 miles of oil shell construction was built from Thunderbolt to the town limits of Tybee, was begun by Chatham County in 1920 and completed in 1923. Construction of five steel bridges over the Wilmington River, Gray's Creek, Turner's Creek, Bull River, and Lazaretto Creek were also begun by Chatham County in 1920 and completed in 1922. The town of Tybee completed the final 1.9 miles of road from the town limits to Butler Avenue in 1924.

The Tybee Road was formally opened on June 21, 1923 with a three day gala celebration that included a variety of events, including a dedication ceremony at the Tybrisa Pavilion, military exhibitions and field events at Fort Screven, "bathing girl" contests, athletic events, and dancing competitions, to name a few. The headlines of that morning's *Savannah Morning News* proclaimed

"Thousands Today Hit Rubber Tires, Officials to Lead Automobile Parade from Savannah to Ocean." The article not only described the events to be held over the coming days, but also predicted the good fortune that the opening of the Tybee Road would bring to the region:

> Fair weather, the open road ahead, a holiday spirit, and the chime of bells and booming of guns, will set the keynote for the great event of today, the dedication of the new Tybee highway, Victory Drive, which will link not only the City of Savannah but the entire state of Georgia to the sea. . . . Not only will it be a Georgia highway, but for the neighboring states of Florida and South Carolina it will offer itself as a route for pleasure and commerce as an integral part of the great Dixie Highway. . . . The drive brings the Atlantic ocean almost to the city's doors.

Victory Drive was named in honor of the soldiers who died on the battlefields of Europe during World War I. It is said that a palm tree was planted for each soldier from Chatham County who died during the "War to End All Wars," making Victory Drive, the area chamber of commerce claimed, "the longest palm tree lined-highway in the country." There is little doubt that the arrival of the 8th Infantry Regiment at Fort Screven in February 1923 had a profound influence on the officials involved with the Tybee Road.

For many in the community the Tybee Road was more than just a road that provided a new means of reaching the island, it was also a point of civic pride. The construction of the road was a testament to the progressive spirit of the people of Savannah and Chatham County, as Tybee was the first barrier island in Georgia to be connected to the mainland by a causeway. With the automobile still relatively new, the construction of a road to Tybee wasn't so much a necessity as it was an expression of the populist individualism of the times. The railroad was still a perfectly functional means of transporting large numbers of people to the resort on Tybee, but Savannahians, demanding greater convenience and independence, pushed for the construction of the road. The Tybee Road allowed Savannahians to come and go as they pleased without regard to train schedules. In addition to convenience, the scenic drive to the island was a source of pride in itself. The automobile allowed people to take in sight seeing on a whole new level, traveling where they wanted to go and seeing what interested them. As a result, auto tourism became the new trend across the nation during the 1920s. In an attempt to attract this new type of tourist, advertisements for the resort such as this from 1930 treated the Tybee Road as an attraction in itself, describing its beauty and its "asphalt surface as smooth as the proverbial glass:"

Tybee is now connected not only with Savannah, but the entire Southeast, by reason of its million dollar paved automobile highway. This road is one of the country's outstanding achievements in road construction and presents a wonderful scenic panorama to the motorist. It is worth a trip to Tybee to travel this smooth beautiful highway. From your own home, wherever you live, you can ride right down to the edge of the pounding surf without getting out of your car.

Another from 1926 claimed that "Victory Drive" was one of the most beautiful highways in the country:

Beginning at Bull Street and Estill Avenue, a broad asphalt boulevard divided in the center by a grass plat lined on either side by rows of stately palmetto palms and gaily colored zinnias and petunias, extends approximately four miles to the township of Thunderbolt. The gay flowers planted by the county and the city authorities have become the delight of thousands of visitors who have taken back to their homes the stories of the beauty of the drive. At Thunderbolt the road leaves the mainland and for fourteen . . . miles this man made ribbon of land extends over a wilderness of islands, marshes, and rivers and connects wooded islets and palm studded hammocks. There are six modern steel draw bridges on the road spanning the rivers . . . the longest of these spans the Bull River which divides Wilmington from the broad marshy savannas of McQueens. At a point several hundred yards northward from the Bull River bridge the drive takes a decided curve and parallels the right of way of the Central of Georgia railway. The highway pass[es] between rows of stately palmettos and graceful oleanders . . . and presents a remarkable spectacle.

As indicated in this *c.* 1925 *Savannah Morning News* article entitled "Tybee Has a Charm and Restfulness All Its Own, and is Aptly Described as Georgia's Playground" (and judging by the title a promotional piece as well), Tybee quickly became a popular destination for auto tourists:

Refugees from the summer heat of the inland allured by her fame, motor hundreds of miles to enjoy the cooling breezes and salty tang of the ocean air. Over the Tybee road in the past year have passed thousands of cars representing half the states in the union. Since the opening of the Savannah River bridge thousands of pleasure seekers from South and North Carolina have motored to the resort, especially over the weekend.

Continued on page 97

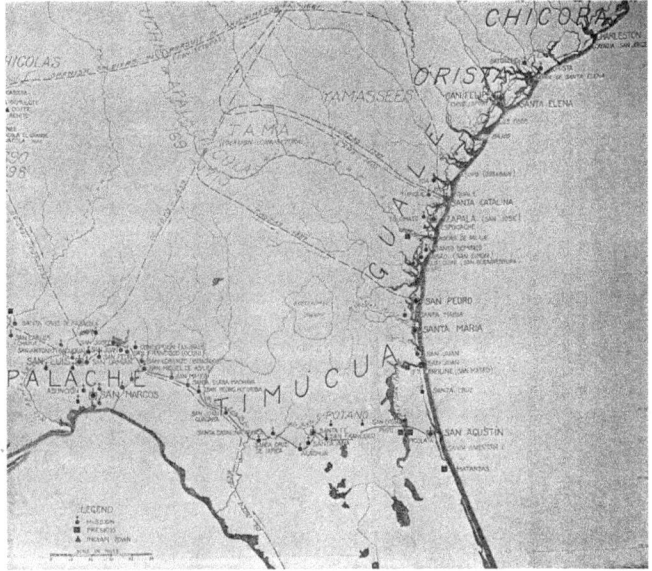

During the seventeenth century La Florida consisted of about 36 missions with at least 10 within the present state of Georgia. Tybee Island, referred to as "Los Bajos" by the Spanish, was between the Spanish frontier town of Santa Elena and the Mission Santa Catalina de Guale on St. Catherines Island.

This 1764 sketch shows Tybee's second lighthouse, built in 1742. The 94-foot structure, which was actually a daymark since it had no light, was replaced in 1773 when it was in danger of being swept away by the tides. (Gamble Collection, Courtesy Bull St. Branch, Live Oak Public Libraries, Savannah, Ga.)

Following Tybee's Union occupation in the fall of 1861, the Martello Tower (c. 1815) on the beach in front of the lighthouse was fortified and garrisoned by the 46th New York State Volunteers. The caption for this sketch from an 1862 New York Herald incorrectly identified the tower as being Spanish. (Gamble Collection, Courtesy Bull Street Branch, Live Oak Public Libraries, Savannah, Ga.)

FORT PULASKI, SAVANNAH RIVER, GEORGIA.—FROM A SKETCH BY AN OFFICER OF THE NAVY.—[SEE PAGE 571.]

Fort Pulaski was the principal defense of the river approach to Savannah and was considered virtually invulnerable to bombardment by both Union and Confederate strategists at the beginning of the Civil War. General Totten, U.S. Army chief of engineers, declared, "you might as well bombard the Rocky Mountains as Fort Pulaski." (Gamble Collection, Courtesy of the Bull Street Branch, Live Oak Public Libraries, Savannah, Ga.)

TYBEE ISLAND, SAVANNAH RIVER, GA. — VIEW OF THE LIGHTHOUSE AND BARRACKS—DESTRUCTION OF THE LIGHTHOUSE BY THE CONFEDERATES, ON ITS EVACUATION.

A raiding party of the Montgomery Guards from Fort Pulaski destroyed a major portion of the Tybee Lighthouse shortly after the Union occupation by igniting a keg of powder on the third floor of the tower. (Gamble Collection, Courtesy Bull Street Branch, Live Oak Public Libraries, Savannah, Ga.)

This photograph of a company of the 46th New York State Volunteers was taken in front of the Martello Tower during the spring of 1862 following the capture of Fort Pulaski. (From the Collection of the Tybee Island Historical Society.)

Battery Lincoln, depicted in this sketch from Harper's Pictorial History of the Civil War, April 1863, was one of a series of 11 batteries constructed on Tybee during the winter of 1862. The construction of the batteries took nearly six weeks, as Union troops transported materials, supplies, ammunition, and ordnance through the surf and across one to three miles of sand and marsh. (Gamble Collection, Courtesy Bull Street Branch, Live Oak Public Libraries, Savannah, Ga.)

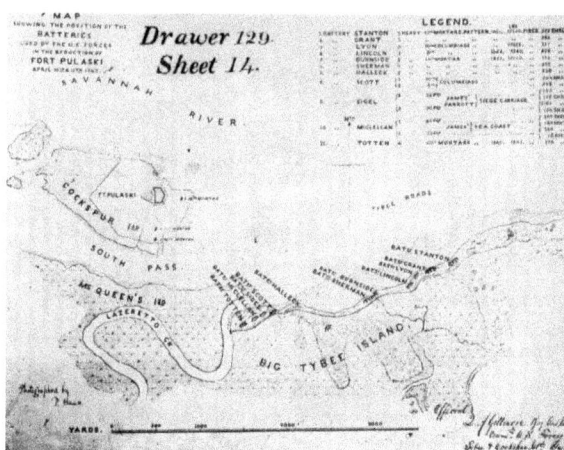

Brigadier General Quincy A. Gilmore drew up a plan for the siege of Fort Pulaski based on his knowledge of the tests of a new weapon, the rifled gun, which the U.S. Army had been experimenting with since 1859. Gilmore concluded that it would be possible to breach the thick walls of Fort Pulaski from Tybee using the new guns. Work on a series of 11 earthwork batteries, mounting 36 guns in all, was begun on February 27, 1862. (From the Collection of Tybee Historical Society.)

This illustration, which appeared in an April 1863 edition of the Harper's Pictorial History of the Civil War, *depicts the jubilant surprise of the Union soldiers at their relatively quick and decisive victory. (Gamble Collection, Courtesy Bull Street Branch, Live Oak Public Libraries, Savannah, Ga.)*

This illustration, which appeared in Frank Leslie's Illustrated Newspaper *on May 3, 1862, depicts the devastating success of the rifled gun in breaching the masonry walls of Fort Pulaski, effectively rendering these types of defenses obsolete. (Gamble Collection, Courtesy Bull Street Branch, Live Oak Public Libraries, Savannah, Ga.)*

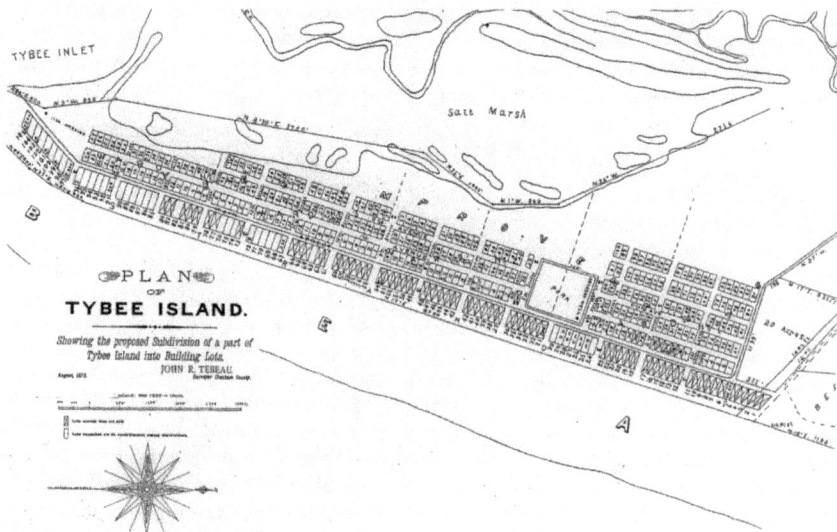

In 1873 a group of Savannah entrepreneurs formed the Tybee Improvement Company for the purpose of promoting the development of Tybee as a seaside resort. This survey, completed by John Tebeau in August 1873, indicates that many of the lots (those marked with an "X") along the oceanfront had already been sold before the plan was printed. (Courtesy of the Tybee Island Historical Society.)

The Atlantic Club was established on the corner of Eighth and Main Streets on Tybee during the late 1880s as a seaside retreat for Savannah Catholics. This photo, taken about 1900, shows club members on the verandah steps of the large two-story building that served as the clubhouse. The building was later used as a boarding house during the 1920s and 1930s and is no longer extant. (Courtesy of Tybee Island Historical Society.)

As seen in this Sanborn Insurance Map for 1888, the completion of the Savannah-Tybee Railroad in 1887 brought on a burst of new development that was concentrated around the Ocean House. (Courtesy Sanborn Map Company.)

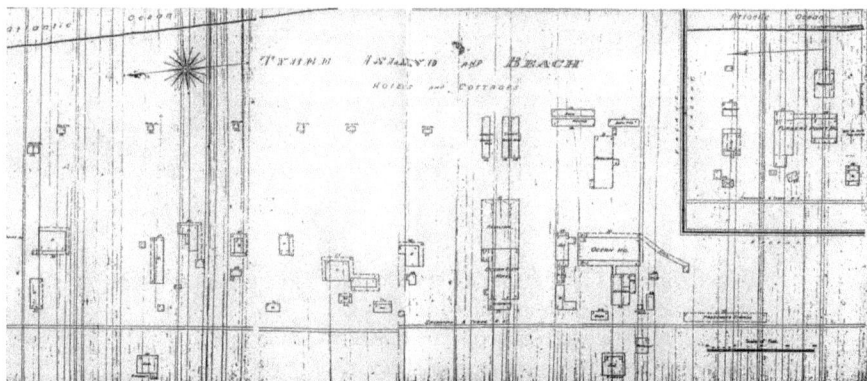

This photo of Hotel Tybee was taken in 1892, about a year after its completion. With over 100 rooms, the new hotel had nearly triple the capacity of the Ocean House. By the turn of the century, Hotel Tybee had become the center of the resort on the island. (Courtesy of Georgia Historical Society, Wilson Collection - VM 1375-2-3-39.)

During the early years of the resort, winter excursions to Tybee were popular. This photograph of a family on the beach at Tybee was taken in December of 1892 (Courtesy Tybee Island Historical Society.)

The Central of Georgia was a key factor in Tybee's development as a major seaside resort during the late nineteenth and early twentieth century. The railroad was an avid promoter of the island through its regional marketing and advertising campaigns, as indicated in this c. 1900 poster for the resort. As a result of Tybee's popularity as a seaside resort destination, the Tybee-Savannah Branch proved to be a very profitable line for the company. (Courtesy Tybee Island Historical Society.)

TYBEE
WHERE OCEAN BREEZES BLOW

EXCURSION RATES
VIA
CENTRAL OF GEORGIA
RAILWAY

The Tybee Inlet Club was built on the corner of Inlet Avenue and 17th Streets about 1895, in close proximity to Inlet Station and the railroad turnstile. Note the open dancing pavilion on the first floor at the rear. This photograph was taken about 1900. (Courtesy of Georgia Historical Society, GHS Collection - 1361PH-18-17-3773.)

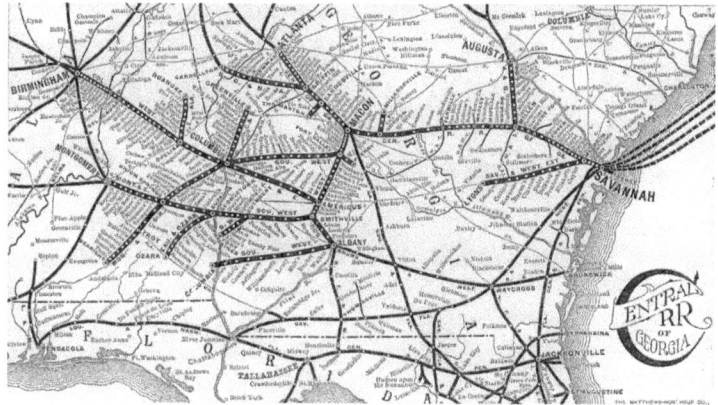

Tybee became a regional resort when the railroad became a unit of the Central of Georgia in 1890, and then under its direct ownership in 1895. This new affiliation gave the island a direct link to hundreds of towns and cities throughout Georgia and Alabama, as depicted on this c. 1895 map. (From Fruits of Industry, Central Railroad of Georgia, c. 1895.)

This Hotel Tybee postcard, postmarked July 5, 1903, was sent to a young lady in Columbia, South Carolina. The scrawled message reads "Arrived o.k. have been pretty lonesome all day. Like Savannah pretty well so far. Residing at #407 Congress Street. Will write tomorrow night. Affectionately, Murray." (Courtesy of Tybee Island Historical Society.)

In an effort to entice people to come to the resort by way of their rail system, the Central of Georgia built the Tybrisa next to Hotel Tybee about 1900. The dance floor and bandstand were in the center of the pavilion, while rocking chairs lined the wraparound verandah on its outer edges. This photo was taken about 1900. (Courtesy of Tybee Island Historical Society.)

This 1909 plat map depicts a section of the Back River area that is sometimes referred to as "Colony Row," a row of cottages built between Inlet Avenue and the mouth of the Back River between 1900–1915. Considered to be one of the most intact concentrations of summer resort architecture in Georgia, Colony Row is an integral part of the Back River Historic District. (Courtesy Howard Reeves.)

A VIEW OF TYBEE INLET COTTAGES

This view of Colony Row was taken from "the Point" and shows the cottages facing the Back River. It was included in a 1925 Tybee Beach Company sales brochure as an example of the type of cottages already built on the island by "men of Southern prominence." (Gamble Collection, Courtesy Bull Street Branch, Live Oak Public Libraries, Savannah, Ga.)

Two Colony Row cottages are pictured in this 1910s photo of the Back River, the Walker-McCall-Lynah Cottage in the center and the Walker-Saussy Cottage on the left. Both were originally owned by Captain George Walker, one of the founders of Strachan Shipping Company. (Courtesy of Tybee Island Historical Society.)

As depicted in this c. 1900 photograph, the Inlet was developed as a more secluded alternative to the frenetic bustle of the resort. The large hip roof house on the right is the Chatham Artillery Club, on the corner of Chatham and Inlet Avenues. Built in 1888, the Chatham Artillery Club was one of the first buildings on the South End. The water tower adjacent the building was part of Inlet Station, where the Central of Georgia trains took on water. (Courtesy of Tybee Island Historical Society.)

The AMFICO Club, pictured here c. 1915, was the corporate retreat of the Atlantic Mutual Fire Insurance Company from about 1915 through the 1930s. Built near the Point as a private summer cottage during the early 1900s, the AMFICO Club is indicative of a distinct type of coastal resort architecture built on Tybee's South End from 1885–1915 and referred to as the "South End Cottage." (Courtesy of Tybee Island Historical Society.)

This c. 1941 War Department map shows what Fort Screven looked like a few years before it was declared surplus at the end of World War II. The prime beach side of the post was reserved for the officers' quarters and staff functions while the less desirable inland side was allocated to the senior NCO and enlisted men. (Courtesy of Tybee Island Historical Society.)

This view of Fort Screven was taken from the lighthouse c. 1907. The long row of buildings facing the ocean at the top is Officer's Row. The grassy expanse between the beach and Officer's Row is the Reviewing Ground. Part of the Senior NCO Row of houses in the post village area is visible on the right. (Courtesy of Tybee Island Historical Society.)

This is a contemporary photo of Building No. 40, the Operations Officers Quarters (c. 1898) located along Officers Row at Fort Screven. Today Officers Row is one of the best preserved sections of the Fort Screven Historic District, listed on the National Register of Historic Places during the 1980s. (Author photo.)

This photo of the 14th Coast Artillery firing a 12-inch mortar at Battery Habersham was taken c. 1908. Battery Habersham, completed in June 1900, contained Fort Screven's greatest medium- and long-range firepower. Featuring a complement of eight mortar pieces, Battery Habersham was manned by seven officers and 219 men. (Courtesy of Tybee Island Historical Society.)

During the early years of World War I, while most of Europe was at war, the troops of the 14th Coast Artillery at Fort Screven kept the post's guns prepared and coordinated land and sea patrols to guard against German U-boat incursions and other subversive activities. In this 1916 photo, the members of the 14th are firing one of Battery Brumby's massive eight-inch rifled guns. (Courtesy of Tybee Island Historical Society.)

Battery Brumby, erected by the Venable Construction Company c. 1897–1898, was the first of six gun emplacements at Fort Screven. This contemporary view of Battery Brumby is of Gun Position #3, one of the last unaltered gun positions at Fort Screven along with Battery Garland, which houses the Tybee Museum. (Author photo.)

This photo of the Martello Tower was taken during the 1910s. Around 1900 the tower was converted for use as the headquarters of the Georgia Telephone and Telegraph Company and later became the site of the new Fort Screven post office. Alice F. Evans, who lived in the GTTC structure on top of the tower, served as postmistress until 1913 when a fire destroyed the post office and her living quarters. The tower was destroyed by the Army Corps of Engineers in 1914 to provide a clear field of fire for Fort Screven's guns. (Courtesy of Tybee Island Historical Society.)

This 1910s photo shows the 72nd Coast Artillery Company firing Battery Gant's two 4.7 inch, rapid fire, anti-torpedo boat guns. Battery Gant required one officer and 25 men to operate. (Courtesy of Tybee Island Historical Society.)

The Post Guard House, constructed about 1900, was just inside the main gates of Fort Screven. Soldiers serving guard duty at various locations throughout the base were quartered in the Guard House during their tour of duty. This photo was taken during the 1910s. Today the building serves as the Tybee Island Community Center. (Courtesy of Tybee Island Historical Society.)

This bird's-eye view of Fort Screven was taken during the 1930s. The four gun emplacements of Battery Brumby are in the foreground while the arc of Officers Row is in the upper left. The Senior NCO Row and village area (which form an L-shape in back of Officers Row) are visible above the five-acre Tybee Light Station in the upper right. (Courtesy of Tybee Island Historical Society.)

In the center of this 1938 photo taken from the top of the lighthouse is the two-story structure that housed the headquarters for District F of the Civilian Conservation Corps, IV Corps Area, from 1933–1939. On the left of the CCC building are two barracks for members of the CCC camp established at Fort Screven. In the background are Battery Garland and Officers Row. (Courtesy of Tybee Island Historical Society.)

This photo of Company B, 1st Battalion, 8th Infantry Regiment was taken on the Reviewing Ground in front of Officers Row during the 1930s. After the Headquarters of the 8th Infantry Regiment were moved from Fort Screven to Fort Moultrie in 1929, the 1st Battalion remained to garrison the post. (Courtesy of Tybee Island Historical Society.)

This c. 1930 photo provides a view of the quartermaster's area from the second floor verandah of the Enlisted Men's Barracks. In the foreground on each side of the palm-lined road are the post bakery and the post exchange. Just visible behind the post exchange is the U-shaped enclosure of the post stables. (Courtesy of Tybee Island Historical Society.)

This photo of Company D, 1st Battalion, 8th Infantry Regiment was taken on the Regimental Parade Ground in front of the twin Enlisted Men's Barracks in 1932. After 17 years at Fort Screven, the 1st Battalion, 8th Infantry Regiment was reassigned to Fort Benning in June 1940. (Courtesy of Tybee Island Historical Society.)

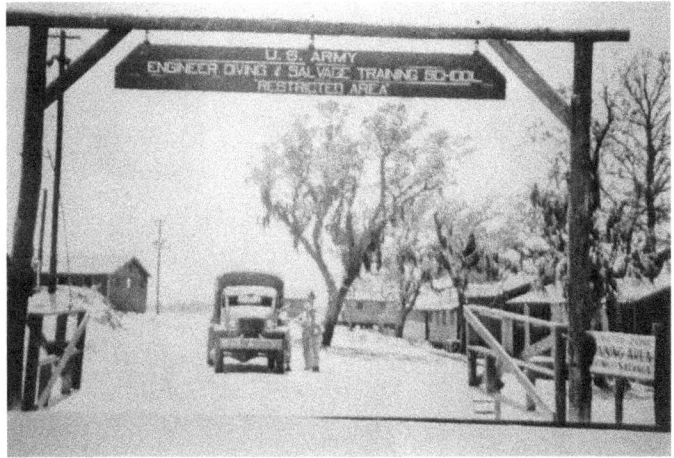

During World War II, Fort Screven became a training command center for the U.S. Corps of Engineers Diving and Salvage Training School. A training camp, shown in this c. 1943 photo, was established near Chimney Creek on the west side of the island off Lewis Avenue. (Courtesy of Tybee Island Historical Society.)

After the original Hotel Tybee was destroyed by fire in 1908, it was replaced in 1911 by this elegant Mediterranean Revival style, three-and-a-half story, 150-room concrete building on the same site. The new Hotel Tybee was the finest hostelry ever built on the island. This c. 1930s photo shows the façade of the building from Main Street. (Courtesy of Georgia Historical Society, Cordray-Foltz Collection - 1360, 18-14-10.)

This photo of Hotel Tybee, "Waiting for Train," was taken about 1920. A covered walkway resembling a pergola connected the hotel to the large, white-columned railroad shed along Main Street, pictured on the left. (Courtesy of Georgia Historical Society, Girard Collection – VM 1374-1-32-02.)

Each spring advertisements in the local paper heralded the approach of the new resort season, which generally began in late May and ended in early September, usually the day after Labor Day. This decorative heading appeared at the top of a full page of advertisements taken out in the Saturday, May 27, 1916 edition of the Savannah Morning News *that featured dozens of the resort's various businesses.*

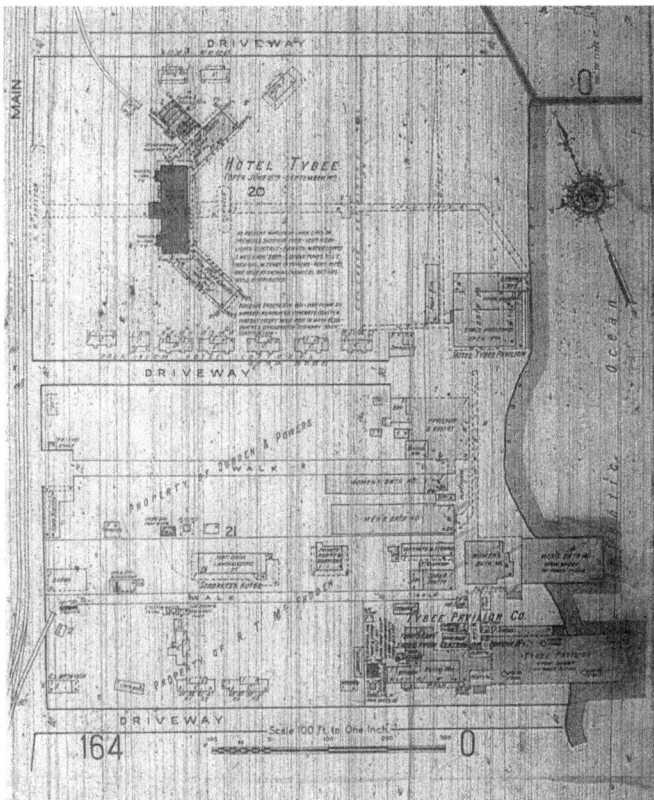

As shown on this c. 1916 Sanborn Insurance Map, Hotel Tybee, Durden and Powers Pavilion, and the Tybrisa Pavilion had become firmly established as the center of the resort on Tybee's South End by the mid 1910s. Vendors set up soda and hotdog stands, bait shops, ice cream stands, cigar shops, amusement and novelty stands, and other small businesses along the walkways from Tybee Station to the pavilions. A wooden boardwalk connected Tybrisa with the Durden and Powers and Hotel Tybee Pavilions, unifying the oceanfront resort area. (Courtesy Sanborn Map Company.)

Tybee's oceanfront pavilion center was not only the center of the resort but also the focal point of municipal life on the island. As seen in this c. 1925 photo, several hundred people have assembled to watch soldiers from Fort Screven march in review on the beach. The municipal boardwalk in the center was in front of Durden and Powers Pavilion. Note the Tybrisa Pavilion in the background. (Courtesy Georgia Historical Society, Girard Collection – VM 1374-1-32-06.)

Taken in 1925, this photo is a typical beach scene showing part of the oceanfront resort area along the boardwalk. The dancing pavilion and restaurant of "The Breakers," formerly Durden and Powers Pavilion, is in the center while the Hotel Tybee Pavilion is on the right. (Courtesy of Georgia Historical Society, GHS Photo Collection - 1361 PH, 18-16-3754.)

The long, bleacher-like steps that lead from the boardwalk in front of the Hotel Tybee Pavilion down to the beach were a favorite place for group photos, like this unidentified gathering in 1915. During the season, the hotel sponsored dances several nights a week in which a good orchestra would provide live music to dance to. (Courtesy of Georgia Historical Society, Cordray-Foltz Collection - 1360, 18-7-7.)

This c. 1920 photo shows the area between the Tybrisa Pavilion and the Tybrisa Bathhouses where a wooden platform provided direct access into the ocean. Tybrisa was so popular that this boardwalk was dubbed "the entrance to the ocean." The walkway from Tybee Station to Tybrisa became the unofficial main street leading to the oceanfront resort area. (Courtesy of Georgia Historical Society, GHS Photo Collection - 1361 PH, 18-16-3747.)

Taken from the Tybrisa Pavilion during the 1920s, this photo shows the beach/ocean access area between the Tybrisa Pavilion and the Izlar Bathhouse, formerly the Tybrisa Bathhouses. During the early 1920s the Central of Georgia Railroad built a new two-story pavilion along 16th Street behind the original Tybrisa. (Courtesy of Georgia Historical Society, GHS Photo Collection - 1361 PH, 18-17-3579.)

This c. 1930 photo provides a view down the crowded walkway from Main Street to the Tybrisa Pavilion. Taken from the Tybrisa boardwalk, Jack Byrnes's concession stand is pictured adjacent the Tybrisa Bathhouse and Restaurant on the left with the columned verandahs of various other concessions on the right. (Courtesy of Tybee Island Historical Society.)

This photo, taken in 1921, is of one of the several concession stands set up along Atlantic Avenue to cater to the throngs of people walking from Tybee Station to Tybrisa and the oceanfront boardwalk of the resort. Many of these stands, with their uniform columns and railings, were built by the resort owners and rented out to vendors. (Courtesy of Tybee Island Historical Society.)

These ads were part of a full-page spread taken out in the Saturday, May 27, 1916 edition of the Savannah Morning News *that highlighted dozens of the resort's various businesses. Note that the ad for Mooney's Place provides its location as "opposite main entrance to ocean."*

This Will be Our 6th Season.   American or European Plan

OCEAN VIEW HOTEL
Bohan's Station **AND RESTAURANT** Tybee Island

F. J. CIUCEVICH, Proprietor

New Furniture—New Addition Built Last Year.

Rooms are Modern—Running Water and Electric Lights Throughout. Rooms With or Without Bath.
The Most Centrally Located Hotel on Tybee Island
Rates $2.00 per day or $12.00 per week
Special Rates by the Month or Table Board to Cottagers
OUR MEALS ARE THE BEST ON THE ISLAND
And will be served again at 50c each. Sea Food and Short Orders a Specialty. Fishing Parties catered to. Reserve your rooms now.

Mooney's Place
TYBEE
OPPOSITE MAIN ENTRANCE TO THE OCEAN.
We Have the Following on Hand:

Cold Drinks		Cigars
Crackerjack	Hot Dogs	Ice Cream
Chewing Gum		Biscuits

Tybee Ice Cream Parlor
Ice Cream Cones and Hot Wieners
Coffee and Sandwiches
SOFT DRINKS
Chocolate Milk and Orange Ade
Crackers, Crackerjack, Peanuts, Cakes, Rolls and Pies
TOBACCOS AND CIGARS

Shooting Gallery
TYBEE
FRONT OF TYBEE PAVILION
Clean Sport
Preparedness-boys

3 Shots for 5c   R. Yamanaka, Prop.

Surf bathers c. 1920s

Although this c. 1925 postcard is an "idealized" birds-eye view of the South End of the island, it does provide an accurate depiction of Hotel Tybee and the oceanfront resort center located along the Strand between 14th and 16th Streets. (Courtesy Tybee Island Historical Society.)

This photo of the Tybee Road, also known as Victory Drive, was taken in the late 1930s. Completed in 1923, Victory Drive was named in honor of the soldiers who died on the battlefields of Europe during World War I. Note the bridge to Fort Pulaski on the left, built in 1938 by CCC camp laborers from Cockspur Island. (Courtesy Georgia Historical Society, Cordray-Foltz Collection – 1360-29-6-01.)

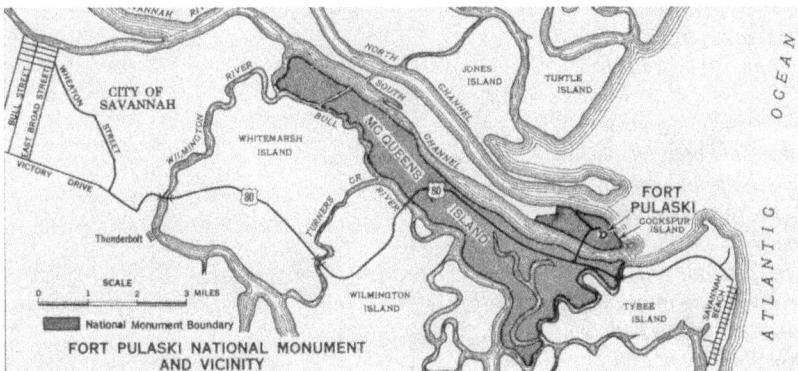

The completion of the Tybee Road in 1923 ushered in a golden era for Tybee as a resort. As indicated on this c. 1950 National Park Service brochure, the Tybee Road, which makes up the eastern end of Highway 80, travels through McQueens Island, which is part of the Fort Pulaski National Monument. (Gamble Collection, Courtesy Bull St. Branch, Live Oak Public Libraries, Savannah, Ga.)

This view south down Main Street from around 14th Street was taken shortly after the completion of the Tybee Road. Note the one-lane shell roads on each side of the railroad tracks. After train service was discontinued in 1933, the rail bed that ran the length of the corridor was made into a palm-lined median and the street was renamed Butler Avenue. Note the railcar in front of the Hotel Tybee train shed. (Courtesy of Georgia Historical Society, Girard Collection – VM 1374-1-32-03.)

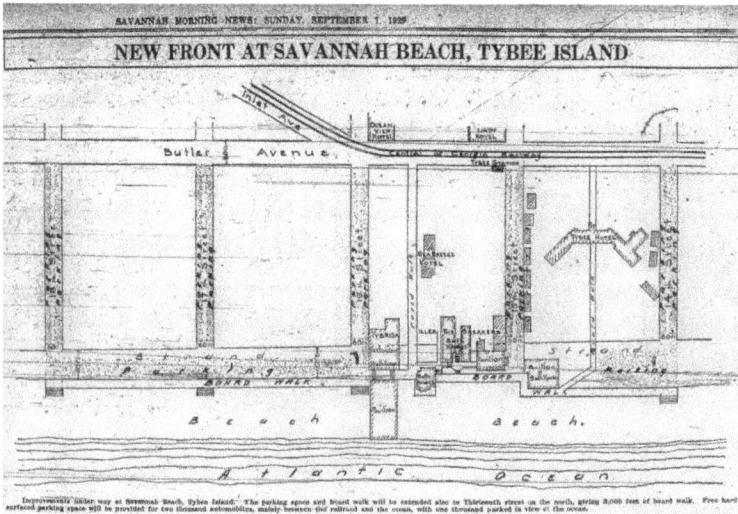

NEW FRONT AT SAVANNAH BEACH, TYBEE ISLAND

This 1929 sketch from the Savannah Morning News illustrates the growth of Tybee's oceanfront resort area, which boasted four hotels, three dance pavilions, four bath pavilions, and dozens of boarding houses and inns. The resort area was joined together by a wooden boardwalk that extended along the beach in front of the Strand from 14th to 18th Streets.

This picture, taken from the Strand near the municipal boardwalk about 1925, gives a view down 15th Street before designated parking areas had been established at the resort. Note the woman reading in the car on the left and the little boy in his bathing suit on the right. After the road was opened people almost immediately began using their cars as bath houses. Note the row of Hotel Tybee cottages along 15th Street in the center, and Hotel Tybee in the background. (Courtesy Georgia Historical Society, Girard Collection – VM 1374-1-32-05.)

This view of the entry platform to the Tybrisa Pavilion (left) and the Tybrisa Bathhouse Building (right) was taken from the municipal boardwalk during the 1920s. Located at "The Entrance to the Ocean," this part of the boardwalk was an ideal place for military recruiters to find young men. Note the open picnic area on the second floor of the Tybrisa Building. (Courtesy Georgia Historical Society, Girard Collection – VM 1374, 1, 32, 12.)

View down Tybee's "Main Street," 16th Street during the 1930s. Note the Tybrisa Pavilion and Bathhouse at left—the huge, 50,000 gallon Tybrisa water tower provided water to the bathhouse, which could accommodate up to 530 patrons a day. This street was the entrance to the largest ocean parkway on the strand, between 16th and 18th Streets. (Courtesy Georgia Historical Society, Girard Collection – VM 1374-1-32-09.)

This photograph, taken shortly after the opening of the Tybee Road in 1923, was taken from the roof of the Tybrisa Pavilion and shows rows of cars parked along a relatively undeveloped 16th Street. Note the open restaurant/picnic area (second floor) of the Tybrisa Building at right. (Courtesy of Tybee Island Historical Society.)

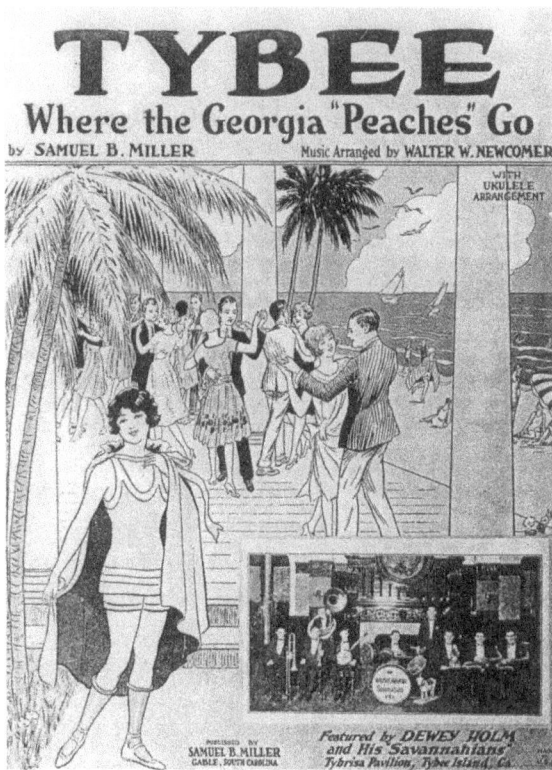

Tybee's renown as a resort was never greater than during the 1920s and 1930s. In 1926 Samuel B. Miller wrote a dance number about Tybee entitled "Tybee: Where the Georgia Peaches Go." The song became a regional hit and was played nightly at the Tybrisa by Dewey Holmes and His "Savannahians." (Courtesy Tybee Island Historical Society.)

This early 1930s photo of the "ocean parkway" adjacent the Tybrisa Pavilion was taken from a boarding house along the Strand between 16th and 17th Streets. The new-found freedom of the auto brought change to the resort in ways that could not have been predicted, such as the decline of public bathhouses. By the late 1930s all but one of Tybee's bathhouses was closed. (Courtesy of Georgia Historical Society, GHS Collection #1361 PH, 18-16-3745.)

The opening of the Tybee Road made it more feasible for year-round living on the island. This photo shows a group of Tybee townspeople in front of the Tybee Town Hall c. 1925. Note the Model-T police car on the left marked "Town of Tybee." The two story building in the background was the original Tybee School built c1900. (Courtesy of Georgia Historical Society, GHS Photo Collection 1361PH-18-17-3758)

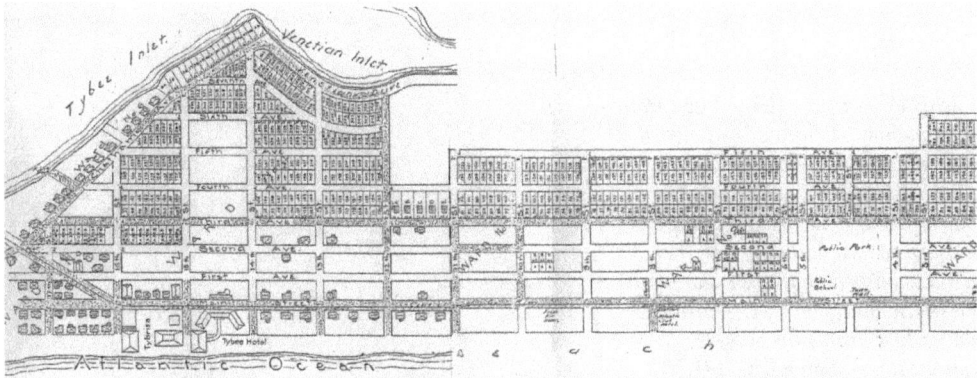

In anticipation of an increased demand for building lots following the opening of the Tybee Road, the Tybee Beach Company commissioned a third subdivision of the island in 1922 (pictured here from a c. 1925 sales brochure). In 1925 the company announced the establishment of a new development, the Venetian Terrace Subdivision, on the southwest end of the island (upper left corner of map).

Around the turn of the century, Fresh Air Homes were established in coastal communities as summer refuges for the poor youth of urban centers. Tybee's Fresh Air Home was established in 1898 by the Froebel Circle. Occupying two full oceanfront lots, the present complex, which was built in 1928, features a main building, four auxiliary buildings, and one of the last pavilions on Tybee. The Fresh Air Home continues its original mission today. (Author photo.)

This photo was taken about 1930 from the very southern tip of Tybee, known locally as "The Point." The AMFICO Club is in the center of the photo between Butler and Chatham Avenues. The observation towers of Hotel Tybee are just visible on the far right. (Courtesy of Georgia Historical Society, Cordray-Foltz Collection #1360, 18-10-01.)

Cletus W. Bergen, AIA—"the Dean of Savannah Architects"—designed a series of "Tybee Cottages" during the 1930s in which he utilized key elements of the Raised Tybee Cottage, a local building type that was established as a design standard for beach houses on Tybee during the early 1930s. One of these commissions, shown here, was for Harry Fulenwider in 1936. (Courtesy of Georgia Historical Society, 1363-339.)

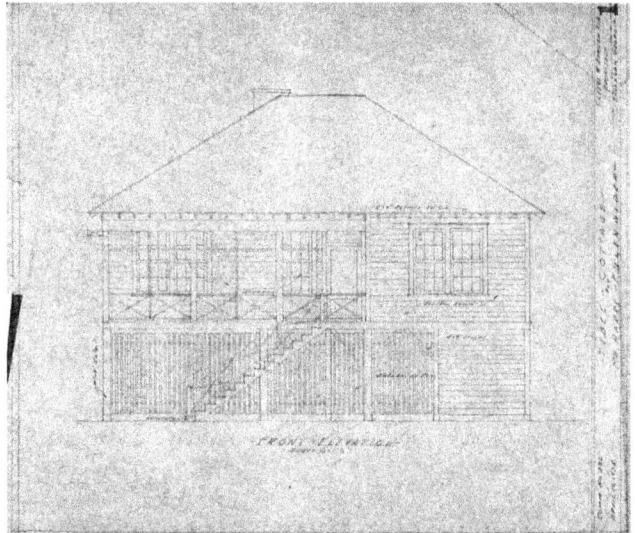

The Dr. Righton Cottage, built on the ocean side of Butler Avenue c. 1930, is a good example of the Raised Tybee Cottage, built on Tybee in great numbers following the completion of the Tybee Road in 1923. The compact shape of the building and its accommodation of the automobile on the ground floor were ideal for the smaller lots that were then being offered. (Author photo.)

Anton Solm built this stylish, two-story oceanfront hotel on the site of the Seaside Cottages. Built during the early 1930s, the Solm's Hotel was one of the most popular of the smaller hotels on Tybee due to its location on the Strand and its proximity to the major resort attractions. This photo was taken c. 1938 after the lower porch was enclosed to create a soda shop and grill. (Courtesy of Tybee Island Historical Society.)

This 1931 photo shows Anton Solm's Seaside Cottages on the corner of Strand and Silver Avenue on fire. Before the end of the day the fire had destroyed over 25 wooden buildings in the boarding house district, the area east of Butler Avenue between 16th and 18th Streets. The photo was taken from the strand parking lot adjacent the Tybrisa. (Courtesy of Tybee Island Historical Society.)

The Carbo House, shown here in a photo taken during the early 1930s, was one of the more substantial boarding houses built during Tybee's golden era as a resort. Built c. 1932 along 16th Street, the Carbo House became a staple hostelry of the resort, providing an inexpensive alternative to the small hotels and inns such as the Ocean View and the Sea Breeze Hotel. Today the Carbo House is one of the few remaining hostelries from the original Tybee resort. (Courtesy of Tybee Island Historical Society.)

This photo of the ocean parkway along the Strand was taken during the late 1930s from the top steps of the Tybrisa Bathhouse. Parking on Tybee was at a premium after the railroad ceased service in 1933. The Solm's Hotel and the Strand Hotel, both established during the 1930s, are visible on the right. (Courtesy of Georgia Historical Society, Cordray-Folz Collection #1360, 18–08–09.)

This bird's-eye view of the Tybrisa Pavilion shows what the resort center looked like during the mid 1930s. The building behind the Tybrisa is the Tybrisa Bathouse and Restaurant, built by the Central of Georgia Railroad during the early 1920s. Adjacent Tybrisa is "The Breakers," formerly Durden and Powers Pavilion and Bathhouse. The long rectangular buildings are bath houses and the gabled building facing the ocean is the dancing pavilion and restaurant. Hotel Tybee is visible in the background. Note the row of Hotel Tybee Cottages along 15th Street. (Courtesy of Georgia Historical Society, GHS Photo Collection #1361 PH, 18-18-3788.)

This photo provides a view of the interior of the Tybrisa Pavilion c. 1940. Note the bandstand in the background and the concession area along the side of the pavilion near the entrance. Civic and social meetings were often held at Tybrisa as it was the largest public space on the island. (Courtesy of Georgia Historical Society, GHS Photo Collection #1361 PH, 18-17-3769.)

This 1940 photo of the Riptide Bar was taken from the ocean parkway. When built in the 1920s, it featured a bathhouse on the first floor and a restaurant on the second floor. By 1940 the bathhouse occupied half the first floor with a dance floor and the Caris Bowling Lanes on the second floor. (Courtesy of Georgia Historical Society, GHS Photo Collection #1361 PH, 18-17-3775.)

This photo, "High Tide at Breakwater," taken along the Strand area in front of Hotel Tybee in 1939, shows the newly completed concrete seawall and oceanwalk built by the WPA in 1938–1939. The seawall and walkway was built along the entire length of the oceanfront resort area from 14th to 18th Streets. The Brass Rail, in the background on the right, was a new nightclub that opened during the 1939 season in a remodeled dancing pavilion/restaurant building, formerly part of the "The Breakers." (Courtesy of Georgia Historical Society, Cordray-Foltz Collection #1360, 18-9-10.)

This photo of Hotel Tybee was taken from Butler Avenue (originally Main Street) in 1941. The five-story towers on each corner of the façade were not ornamental, but were intended to be used as observation towers for hotel patrons. Where the palm tree-lined walkway is located in the photo there was once a covered boardwalk that connected the entrance of the hotel and the massive railroad shelter that stretched along the tracks of the Central of Georgia Railroad. (Courtesy of Georgia Historical Society, Cordray-Foltz Collection #1360, 18-15-01.)

Completed in 1940 on the island's North End, the Desoto Beach Hotel and Cabana Club was the last major hostelry built on Tybee. The complex was affiliated with the Desoto Hotel in Savannah and featured a clubhouse and two "Mediterranean style villas" to accommodate guests. This view of the hotel complex was taken from the dunes adjacent the parking lot c. 1945. The clubhouse is on the right and Villa Adeline and Villa Caroline are on the left. (Courtesy of the University of Georgia, Albertype Company Collection MS #1299.)

View of Desoto Beach Club from the beach c. 1940s. (Courtesy Tybee Island Historical Society.)

This aerial view of a part of the resort was taken c. 1958. Along the beach is the "ocean parkway" and in the center, far right, Tybrisa is just visible along 16th Street. The long gable building above Tybrisa is the Seabreeze Hotel. Along the Strand across from the ocean parkway, the Solms and Strand Hotels are seen almost in the center (the Solms is adjacent the cars parked in an arc). Along the left is 17th Street, the heart of the boarding house district. In the background, in the upper left, the Back River is just visible. (Courtesy of Tybee Island Historical Society.)

This c. 1954 Sanborn Fire Insurance map illustrates how the resort had changed since the 1920s. Of the three original pavilions, the Tybrisa was the only one that remained in its original form. Hotel Tybee remained relatively unchanged since its completion in 1911 but was demolished in 1961 as part of a redevelopment of the site. The north wing, which was remodeled into the 22-room Tybee Motel in 1958, is the only part of the hotel that remains today. (Courtesy Sanborn Map Company.)

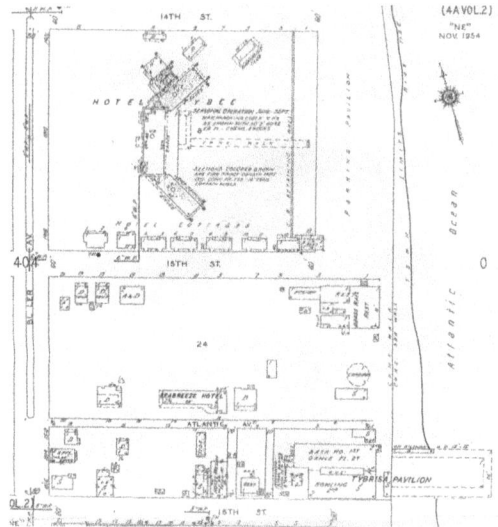

During the 1940s several fishing camps were established along the Back River near Horse Pen Creek (renamed "Venetian Inlet" during the 1920s). This photo, taken during the 1950s, is a view of one of the fishing camps located at the mouth of Horse Pen Creek at the north end of Chatham Avenue. The camp later became the Tybee Marina. (Courtesy of Tybee Island Historic Society).

By the early 1950s the resort on Tybee began to decline in popularity, although it was still a summer destination for Georgians. The cover of this c1961 Savannah Beach Chamber of Commerce brochure was actually recycled from a 1930 brochure, perhaps in an attempt to evoke the resort's golden era.

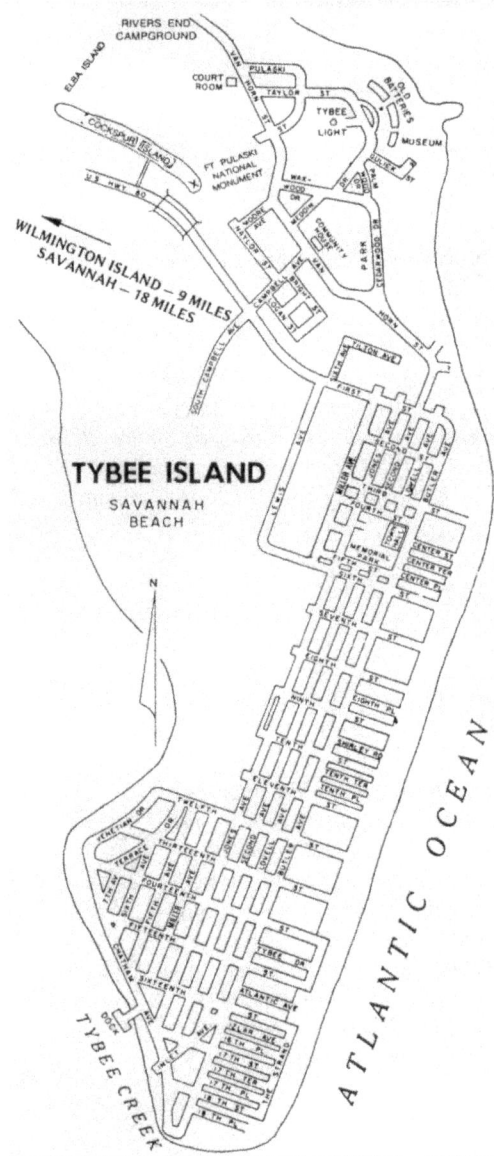

1976 Location Map of Savannah Beach, Tybee Island.

Continued from page 64

Georgia's Playground

The completion of Tybee Road ushered in a golden era for Tybee as a resort. As proclaimed in a *c.* 1925 brochure, Tybee was now the "the accessible playground of 8,000,000 people of the Southeast, and the queen of the South Atlantic coast resorts." As a result of the island's increased accessibility, the resorts flourished during the mid 1920s and early 1930s, and Tybee entered into an unparalleled building boom. Rows of boarding houses and numerous small hotels were established to accommodate the crush of people visiting the island. It was during this time that Cab Calloway and other Big Band personalities performed at Tybee's dancing pavilions. With more people visiting the island than ever before, Tybee was arguably the most popular summer beach resort on the south Atlantic coast during this period.

During the 1920s Tybee's oceanfront resort area had grown to include four hotels, three dance pavilions, four bathhouse pavilions, and dozens of boarding houses and inns. In addition to Hotel Tybee, the Seabreeze Hotel, and the Ocean View Hotel, there was now the Lindy Hotel (*c.* 1925), on the corner of 15th and Main Streets, opposite Tybee Station. Although the three major dance pavilions at the resort center remained relatively the same, the Central of Georgia Railroad (which later sold the Tybrisa property to the Tybrisa Pavilion Company in 1926) built a new two story restaurant and bath house behind the original Tybrisa Dance Pavilion during the early 1920s. The new building contained a large bath house on the first floor and a restaurant with wraparound verandah on the second floor. The new Tybrisa Bathhouse featured 325 rooms for men and 205 rooms for women. Tybrisa advertisements maintained that the rooms were all large and airy and that the bathhouse was one of the finest on the Atlantic coast: "It is equipped with numerous shower baths, sterilizing machinery for bathing suits and towels. A 50,000-gallon tank furnishes pure, fresh water for shower baths, etc."

The old Tybrisa bath houses, adjacent the Tybrisa Dancing Pavilion at the end of Atlantic Avenue, became the Izlar Bathhouse, which featured 75 rooms for men and 75 rooms for women. Together with the Hotel Tybee and Durden and Powers Bathhouses, the resort front had a total of 1,095 bath rooms for men and 685 for women in 1925, giving the resort the capability to accommodate up to 1,800 bathers a day. Lifeguards were employed by each of the bath houses to patrol the beach during hours of operation. On weekends and holidays the Red Cross Life Saving Corp provided additional life guards to the resort.

Tybee's boarding house district developed south of the resort center between 16th and 18th Streets, and featured an assortment of boarding houses and rental cottages that were available for rent by the week, month, or season. These establishments offered a less expensive and more casual alternative to Hotel Tybee and the other smaller hotels. Of the boarding houses established in the district by this time, the Carbo House (*c.* 1925) on 16th Street and the Izlar Boarding House (*c.* 1910s) on Izlar Avenue were among the most popular and well known, and were places where small groups of people would gather after hours. Other boarding houses in the district included the Tybee Beach House and the Perkins House. Anton Solm's Seaside Cottages on the corner of Strand and Izlar Avenue were among the several dozen cottages available for rental within the boarding house district and along the Back River. All these establishments were within two blocks of "the Front," as the main resort area was sometimes called.

To accommodate auto tourism, new streets were opened and "ocean parkways" were created along the strand areas in front of Hotel Tybee and the boarding house district. Original plans presented in 1929 announced a phased project to be completed by the 1935 season. The plan called for the hard surfacing of 14th through 18th Streets between the railroad and the Strand, as well as the creation of hard surfaced, oceanfront parking along the Strand between 16th and 18th Streets south of the Tybrisa Pavilion, and between 15th and 13th Streets north of the Tybrisa. The plan would provide free parking for a total of 3,000 automobiles, accommodating 2,000 automobiles "mainly between the railroad and the ocean, with one thousand parked in plain view of the ocean." In addition, the resort area would be connected by a 3,000-foot wooden boardwalk that would extend along the beach in front of the Strand from 18th to 13th Street. Between 1929 and 1932, half of this plan had been implemented, resulting in the hard surfacing of 14th through 17th Streets and the creation of ocean parkways along the Strand between 14th and 15th Streets and 16th and 17th Streets. As provided for in the plan, a boardwalk was constructed that extended 1,500 feet along the beach from 14th to 17th Streets, joining the completed sections of the project. At the opening of the 1932 season, Tybee's oceanfront resort center could accommodate up to 1,500 automobiles. During this time, Tybee was the only resort north of Florida that offered free oceanfront parking.

Prohibition on Tybee

During the 1920s and early 1930s, Prohibition bred an undercurrent of illicit activity throughout the United States. It is little coincidence that

Tybee's golden era as a resort coincided with Prohibition. In addition to providing seaside attractions for the family, other entertainments were available in the back rooms of Tybee's pavilions, restaurants, and boarding houses. Bootleg liquor and homemade moonshine was readily available to resort patrons while Durden and Powers and the various casinos that were established offered slot machines in the front rooms and poker, blackjack, and craps in the back.

During this time, Tybee was notorious not only for its "watering holes," but also for its role as a conduit for smuggling liquor into the country. The speakeasies and drawing rooms of Savannah, as well as much of the state, were supplied through Tybee. It has been said that the basements of some of the finest houses along Victory Drive in Savannah were used as storehouses for bootleg liquor brought in through Tybee during this time. According to Elizabeth Carpenter Piechocinski in *Once Upon an Island*, the Prohibition era gave rise to the "Bootleg Princes" who "operated fleets of fast cutters between the West Indies and Tybee Island." In fact, one of the biggest smugglers in the country, Anthony Cassese, the so-called "King of the Bootleggers," was arrested in Savannah in 1922 by federal officers on the charge of transporting whiskey from the Bahamas and bringing it through Tybee Island, where the contraband liquor would be distributed throughout the country. Cassese was later extradited to New York where there was a previous warrant for his arrest in Brooklyn.

Far more common than the big-time bootleggers like Cassese were the small operators who navigated the narrow creeks and small rivers around Tybee and other nearby islands. Tybee's Back River was often used as a safe harbor for rum runners, who would smuggle in small caches of liquor from Cuba and the Caribbean on small boats and skiffs. Arrests for smuggling were frequent, as illustrated by this incident on Tybee in 1927. The headline of the *Savannah Morning News* article detailing the bust read "Fine Assortment of Liquor Taken—Federal Officers Make Haul in Tybee Inlet— Arrest One —Charge Receiving, Concealing, Smuggling."

The article gives a decidedly "Victorian" description of the types of liquor seized and gives a good account of the type of raids that were conducted on Tybee and in Savannah during America's "Peculiar Experiment:"

> A collection of liquors, of a kind which makes some people jump
> up and down in ecstasy, and makes others find their throats growing
> excessively parched and thirsty, was seized by federal agents and deputy
> marshals on Tybee Island in the inlet yesterday morning.

[The accused] is charged with receiving, concealing, and smuggling into the country 400 cases of assorted liquors, ranging from choice champagne to choice gin, and including Scotch and rye whisky. There was also found by the officers some beer of particularly appetizing appearance, and, according to their declaration, of a kind which seldom touches the Georgia shore.

The estimated value of the seizure, rated at the lowest cost price across the water, would be approximately $6,000, allowing for each case to average $15 in cost. At retail, such an assignment of liquors would triple and sometimes quadruple in price, the grade of those seized being declared by the officers to have been of an exceptional kind. The raiding party left Savannah just before midnight Friday and made the seizure Saturday morning. They returned to Savannah at 3:00 yesterday afternoon.

Dancing Days

Following the end of World War I, social life on Tybee began to change. During the 1910s young ladies of the community generally lived the way their mothers and grandmothers had lived, observing a very strict standard of social conduct. Young ladies summering on Tybee "would live on the beach in the mornings, had . . . social duties in the afternoon, and went to the dances at the Tybee Hotel Pavilion" in the evenings. In recalling those times, one Savannahian maintained that "we were very proper in those days," adding that "girls went to the formal dances with their chaperones, had their dance cards filled out before the big evening, but there was always time for 'fresh air' on the beach between the dances."

By the end of the 1920s, however, the strict Victorian practices of the early 1900s had given way to the progressiveness of the Roaring Twenties. Fueled by the roadhouses and speakeasies of the Prohibition era and the spirit of individualism spawned by the infancy of auto culture, the bawdy, fast paced environment exhibited at the resort on Tybee during the 1920s and 1930s was in stark contrast to the resort's more familial atmosphere at the turn of the century. Coming of age in an era of great technological innovation and prosperity, young ladies of the era responded to the fast-paced 1920s by going to the beach to dance at the resort's pavilions. The pavilions would sponsor dances every night during the summer season except on Sundays. Six- and twelve-piece orchestras hired by the pavilions would provide a program of dance music each night. Although the Savannah-Tybee branch of the Central of Georgia was still the most popular method of transportation to and from the dances during the late 1920s, more and more young people began to pool their gas money together to go by car in order to avoid the last minute rush for the 12:15 a.m. train back to Savannah.

During the 1930s admission to the dances at Hotel Tybee and Tybrisa was about 50 cents, although "depression dances" were also held at the Tybrisa for a mere 15 cents. The dance floor at Tybrisa was well known for its enormous "crystal ball" that hung from the ceiling, "revolving slowly with bright beams of light reflected from its mirrors and small pieces of glass." On Tuesday nights the "college tag dances" were popular and well attended, while amateur groups, barbershop quartets, and small musical organizations would sometimes provide impromptu performances on the beach near the pavilions for the sheer enjoyment of entertaining.

The early 1930s spawned the era of the touring Big Bands, which would usually make a Friday or Saturday night appearance at the Tybrisa, by then Georgia's largest and best known dancing pavilion. The local bands would play during the week. Both Tybrisa and the Hotel Tybee Pavilion featured a six piece orchestra that provided music for dancing every afternoon and evening and concert music on Sunday afternoon. Bob Sheppard's Moonlight Serenaders were very popular with the younger crowds at the Tybrisa during this time. Al Cutter, Raymond Snype, and John Phillips also lead "bands in residence" during this period. On the weekends national touring acts would come to Tybee to play "one night stands." Many of the famous band leaders of the day have related the ordeal of traveling by bus to get to the next night's town, getting a few hours sleep, then going to the local hall, usually a pavilion like the Tybrisa, playing for the evening, and repeating the process all over again. During this time the Tybrisa was on par with the finest pavilions of the east coast, and was part of the touring circuit between New York City and Miami that included some of the most renowned venues in the country, such as Atlantic City's Steel Pier. The greatest bands in the country came to perform at the Tybrisa, including Cab Calloway, Bob Crosby and The Bobcats, Guy Lombardo and the Royal Canadians, The Benny Goodman Orchestra, the Ted Weems Orchestra, Louis Prima, Louis Armstrong, Glenn Miller, and Tommy and Jimmy Dorsey, among others.

Tybee's notoriety as a resort was never more acclaimed than during the Big Band era of the late 1920s and early 1930s. The spirit of the times was captured in both song and in words. In 1926 Samuel B. Miller, a songwriter from South Carolina, was inspired to write a dance number about the island called "Tybee: Where the Georgia Peaches Go." The song, which became a regional hit, was played nightly at the Tybrisa by Dewey Holmes and His Savannahians:

> Let us sing of lovely beaches,
> And those pretty Georgia peaches,
> Down at Tybee.
>
> Laughing eyes with love a glowing,
> Pearly teeth twixt red lips showing,
> Down at Tybee.
>
> It was there a peach I courted,
> As we splashed around and sported,
> Where I slyly stole sweet kisses,
> Oh those charming, thrilling blisses,
> Down at Tybee.
>
> Chorus:
> Tybee, Tybee Where the Georgia Peaches Go
> Tybee, Tybee Where the Ocean Breezes Blow
> On the dance pavilion with your sweet
> You feel like a million, while you shake your feet

Conrad Aiken, a famous author and native Savannahian, wrote a short story during this time that drew on his experiences growing up in Savannah. Aiken's "Strange Moonlight," which was published in 1926, portrayed a Savannah family's outing to Tybee Island in which he described the pavilions and numerous amusements that were available to day-trippers. Aiken also provided one of the best descriptions of the scenic train ride, which would later be remembered by Savannahians as one of the most lauded and cherished memories of the early resort:

> They climbed into the funny, undignified little train, which almost immediately was lurching over red-iron bridges enormously complicated with girders and trusses. Great excitement when they passed the gray stone fort, Fort Pulaski . . . a cloud shadow, crossing it, made it somber . . . He looked out at the interminable green marshes, the flying clouds of rice-birds, the channels of red water lined with red mud, and listening to the strange complex rhythm of the wheels on the rails and the prolonged melancholy wail of the whistle.

The Golden Era

In addition to attaining new heights as a resort, Tybee also came of age as a municipality during the 1920s. Although the town was incorporated in 1887, its affairs had been largely controlled by the early developers throughout the late nineteenth and early twentieth centuries. Perhaps as a consequence of its dealings with the Savannah city council and the Chatham County board of commissioners during the planning and construction of the Tybee Road, the elected officials of the Town of Tybee were much more visible as a governing body after the road opened in 1923. As a result of the new growth on the island, the town government found itself with greater responsibilities. It addition to providing increased police protection, the town initiated a road building program to accommodate the crush of auto tourists visiting the island. By 1925 Tybee had four miles of asphalt streets, four miles of graded unpaved streets, and a new two mile, shell boulevard named Butler Avenue (formerly Main Street) under construction. The town had also recently purchased an artesian waterworks system, had its own electric light system, and operated a graded public school.

Naturally, the emergence of an active mayor and council was seen as another way to market the resort. An able municipal government would make people that were considering building a summer cottage on Tybee feel more secure in their investment. A nurturing civic atmosphere would encourage others to make Tybee their home, and in turn, the establishment of a larger year-round population would bolster lot sales and make it possible to establish Tybee as a year-round resort. In order to accomplish these ends, advertisements for the resort during the mid to late 1920s portrayed the Town of Tybee as a progressive seaside community, the first time Tybee was identified in tourism-related literature as a "town" rather than just a resort development:

> Tybee is a regularly incorporated municipality, governed by a mayor and board of alderman, who have seen to it that Tybee has kept pace in all modern ways with its recent growth. For Tybee considers itself more than a summer resort, and its farsighted citizens have made plans accordingly.

Another pointed out that the town included the entire island with taxes paid on an assessed value of approximately $1 million:

> It is the most democratic community and selects citizens of ability and initiative to handle its affairs . . . It has an efficient police system, rigidly

enforced sanitary laws and has accomplished wonders in community development . . . Pride, patriotism, and progressiveness are always in evidence at Tybee.

At first the town used the allure of its new automobile road as a means to encourage the construction of summer cottages for families to spend the season on the island, as seen in this section of a *c.* 1925 promotional brochure for the Town of Tybee and the Tybee Beach Company:

> Many of the most prominent and influential citizens of the towns adjacent Savannah, have invested in Tybee homes and send their wives and children to Tybee for the summer months, while they remain at home to carry on business affairs, but the excellence of the road, between their homes and Tybee, permits them to spend weekends and holidays with their families and enjoy the many pleasures which Tybee affords.

For Savannahians, however, the idea of spending the summer at the beach during the resort season was not a new concept, as it was practiced from the very beginnings of the resort. The construction of the automobile highway, however, made summering much more practical by making the island more accessible. It was now possible for a gentleman to make the daily commute between Savannah and Tybee, conducting business in the city during the mornings and afternoons while spending the evenings and nights on Tybee with his wife and children. A summer cottage on Tybee was now a more realistic investment as it could be more fully utilized as a second home. As a result, it became fashionable during the 1920s and 1930s among Savannah's upper middle class to own a summer cottage on Tybee. Each year families would return to their summer cottage to spend the season, commonly from late May to early September, a practice that would be perpetuated by subsequent generations.

It was during this time that the classic summer cottages, or "Raised Tybee Cottages," which became so characteristic of the island, were built. As building lots were at a premium, almost all the remaining oceanfront lots along Butler Avenue were subdivided into several smaller parcels to meet the growing demand. The smaller cottages that were built at this time were raised a full story to allow for the accommodation of auto storage on the ground level. By the early 1930s there were over 400 privately owned cottages on the island.

By the end of the 1920s the Town of Tybee had a small but significant year-round population of about 200 people. In an effort to increase the visibility of Tybee as both a summer resort destination and increasingly as a viable year-round "beach town," the Town of Tybee changed its name to the "Town of Savannah Beach, Tybee Island, Georgia" in 1929. Because Savannah was well known throughout the country it was thought that a closer association with the city would increase visitation and encourage further growth. Also, the connotation that Tybee was "Savannah's Beach" provided the illusion of proximity, suggesting that Tybee was within an easy drive of the "Hostess City of the South."

In an effort to sustain the building boom of the 1920s that followed the completion of the Tybee Road and the unparalleled popularity of the resort's dancing pavilions and other boardwalk amenities, the Town of Savannah Beach continued to advertise Tybee as an ideal seaside cottage community with the amenities of a real year-round municipality. As evidenced in this *c.* 1930 promotional brochure, the substitution of the words "home" and "residence" in place of "cottage" is a subtle indication of the direction the town was moving in:

> Savannah Beach, Tybee Island, Georgia, is winning recognition over a large territory as one of the most desirable seaside resorts in the South for home-builders. A number of very attractive residences have recently been erected, not only by Savannahians but by lovers of the seaside in other cities. Sales of lots indicate a very large building program in the future. Building lots of an adequate size are sold at reasonable prices, and building costs are moderate. Paved highways lead to all residences, and the Town of Savannah Beach co- operates in every possible way with its property owners.

Although there is little doubt that the municipality welcomed the investment of the summer residents, the establishment of a permanent population on Tybee would serve to stabilize the community as well as the economy of the island, the prosperity of which was almost completely reliant on the success of the yearly resort season. The Tybee Road now made living on Tybee more practical as the travel time between the island and the mainland was nearly cut in half. By 1930 the Town of Savannah Beach and the development companies were publishing promotional brochures that encouraged people to make Tybee their home:

> You can live at Tybee the year-round and live economically. Convenient transportation either by train or automobile will connect you with your business almost as quickly as though you lived in the city. You can make your fortune in beautiful, progressive Savannah and

maintain your home on Tybee beach, insuring health, happiness, and longevity to you and your loved ones. Property at Tybee is pronounced by experts to be "the best buy." Own a little home on Tybee Island. It will be a source of life-long pleasure and the best heritage you could leave for those who come after you. Tybee is a cultured, law abiding community built around home atmosphere and owes its phenomenal growth to a solid citizenry who seek that high citizenship that follows sunshine, health, and out of door pleasures. If you are not a "regular" citizen of Tybee, you are invited to become one. There is no stranger within our gates. As a citizen you become one of a delightful colony and participate in every civic endeavor.

Perhaps one of the most ambitious real estate ventures during this time was the development of the Venetian Terrace Subdivision. By the early 1920s, many of the building lots made available through the Tybee Beach Company as a result of the *c.* 1890 subdivision of the island had been sold. Most of the remaining undivided land that the company owned was salt marsh on the south end of the island, between Horse Pen Creek and Third Street. In order to develop this land, the Tybee Beach Company filled in the area south of 12th Street during the early- to mid-1920s. The 88 acres that resulted were subdivided into lots and the development was called Venetian Terrace. The company also controlled the sale and development of the lots north of 12th Street, between Third and Sixth Avenues. A company brochure outlined plans for the subdivision:

> The new development will have a beautiful boulevard circling the entire subdivision, running along the waters of Tybee Inlet (Chatham Avenue), then turning on the shore of Venetian Inlet back into the paved street, Third Avenue. This boulevard (Venetian Drive) will be a beautiful thoroughfare, bordered on either side with palmetto trees and flower plats.
>
> Venetian Inlet (also known as Horse Pen Creek), bordering on the western side of this property, has been dredged out to be used as a protective yacht basin and could accommodate several hundred boats. There will be a public dock, insuring everyone access to and from their boats. This in addition to the present docking facilities now to be had on the Inlet, namely the municipal dock, insures every possible convenience for boating and yachting parties.

By the mid 1930s Tybee had a permanent population of around 350 and a substantial number of year-round residences had been built on the island.

During the summer, when the cottage owners returned for the resort season, the population would swell to 6,000. About this time the intersection of 16th Street and Butler Avenue began to develop as the main commercial area where much of the daily business of the town was conducted. A bus station, post office, department stores, grocery stores, and other businesses were established not only to cater to the visiting summer resort crowd, but also for the year-round residents.

Chapter Six

WEATHERING CHANGE

Despite the overwhelming popularity of the resort and the great boom in development that followed the completion of the Tybee Road, the coming of the automobile did have some adverse effects on Tybee, eventually bringing about the demise of several old staples of the resort.

E. B. Izlar, one of Tybee's early civic leaders during the island's pioneer days, recounted some of the changes brought on by the automobile in an article published in the April 17, 1931 edition of the *Savannah Evening Press* entitled "E. B. Izlar, 58 Years Old Today, Has Spent 30 Years on the Island—Recalls the 'Good Ol' Days' at the Beach." The article quotes Izlar as listing the "decline of mosquitoes, of picnickers, of bars, and of yardage of women's bathing suits" as the most radical changes of the past 30 years on the island, attributing the decline in "the picnicking habit among Americans" and "bath house bathing" directly to the automobile. He commented that in the "good old days," people would look forward to substantial "outings" a few times a year. Now people could have picnics out of their cars twice a day if they desired. In reference to the use of bath houses, Izlar pointed out that "many people [are] coming down in suits or using their cars as bath houses." People simply drove home in wet clothes rather than change, since they did not have to board the train or return to a boarding house or hotel. As a result of these changes, use of the over 1,800 bath house units available at Tybee's pavilion center declined sharply. By the end of the 1930s, the Tybrisa Bathhouse was the only bathhouse on Tybee that remained in operation. The decline in the picnic habit combined with the decline in bath house bathing eventually led to the closing of both the Hotel Tybee Pavilion and The Breakers Pavilion. Since the resort's dancing pavilions also doubled as picnic pavilions during the day, the decline in picnicking also contributed to the decline in use of both of these pavilions. As the Tybrisa had largely absorbed the remaining market for bath house amenities and picnic facilities, and was already by far the most popular dance pavilion, Tybee had become a "one pavilion resort" by the opening of the 1939 season.

End of the Line

Of all the changes brought on by the Tybee Road, the eventual discontinuation of rail service to the island is certainly the most remembered and perhaps the most regretted. Although the Central of Georgia continued service to Tybee for 10 years following the completion of the road, ceasing operation in 1933, the closing of the Tybee route was practically assured the first day the road opened. The prevailing attitude among the developers of the resort and the municipal government after 1923 was that the future of the island rested with the automobile and that the railroad, while still useful, was not modern and therefore "old hat." A *c.* 1930 brochure for the town and resort, which highlighted the Tybee Road and the "progressiveness" of the Town of Savannah Beach, underscores this sentiment. The brochure points out that the Tybee Road is the perfect "approach" to the resort, listing its attributes compared to its predecessor:

> With the finest automobile highway leading to any seashore resort on the South Atlantic coast . . . Savannah Beach, Tybee Island, Georgia had the superb advantage of an approach befitting its charms. . . . With the many millions of dollars yearly expended on automobile highways in the country directly tributary to this famous resort . . . it can be accurately said that all public roads of the Southeast now point and lead to Savannah Beach, and that from hundreds of thousands of homes access to Tybee Island is direct and comfortable and speedy.

The brochure went on to make a direct comparison between the speed and comfort afforded those traveling to the island by automobile rather than by train. It even insinuated a difference in social class between the auto owner and "those that are not auto owners," and were therefore left with only the train as an option:

> Two million white population can reach Savannah Beach by automobile in far less time and with far greater comfort than a few thousand could not many years ago. To those who are not automobile owners exceptional railway facilities, with low summer excursion rates, offer opportunity to visit this resort, either for single day trips or week-end visits, or for more prolonged enjoyment of its unceasing pleasures. . . . and the passenger tariffs are proportionately as low as any of the outstanding resorts of the North. Many thousands every season regularly avail themselves of these splendid facilities and this railroad

service continues to be a great contributing factor in the welfare and development of the resort.

This reference to rates being "proportionately as low as any of the outstanding resorts of the North" and the declaration that the railroad "continues to be a great contributing factor in the welfare and development of the resort" are references to plans for marketing Tybee as a year-round resort. With the widespread ownership of automobiles and the construction of good highways connecting the resort to other regional population centers, it was thought that the Tybee Road would sustain the resort as a regional attraction. Continued growth, however, would depend on attracting snow birds from the north and landlocked tourists from the Midwest, making long distance transportation such as a railroad system a necessary option. Although the Town of Savannah Beach was becoming a year-round community with a growing permanent population, the resort had failed to develop a year-round tourist clientele. Major hostelries such as Hotel Tybee would continue to close down for the winter and many of the island's resort-related businesses would be mothballed until the beginning of the next season. The railroad was a necessary ingredient for Tybee to make the successful transition from a largely regional, southern resort to a more cosmopolitan resort operating on a national scale.

The failure of Savannah Beach to become a true year-round resort and "playground" is directly linked to the municipal government's inability to create an environment to sustain the railroad. The investment of municipal dollars was prioritized to provide the infrastructure necessary to accommodate the automobile—the construction of roads, driveways, and oceanfront parking dramatically changed the landscape of the island. The long lines of cars both traveling and parked along Butler Avenue made it difficult for the train to make stops and to turn around at Inlet Station. By 1930 the Central of Georgia was losing money on the Tybee route. As a cost saving measure, the railroad began running buses to Tybee in place of steam trains during the winter of 1930, a development that was announced in the November 1930 issue of the *Central of Georgia Magazine*:

> Bus service operated by the Central of Georgia Motor Transport Company has replaced steam train service on our Tybee District . . . plans contemplate the re-establishment of steam train service between Savannah and Tybee in the spring or early summer of 1931. Bus service is being operated during the winter months when travel by

train decreases and passenger receipts on the Tybee District are not
sufficient to pay operating expenses.

Despite efforts to sustain service between Tybee and Savannah, the Central
of Georgia was ultimately unable to compete with the automobile and in 1933
rail service to Tybee was discontinued. The public's reaction to the Central of
Georgia's announcement was met with a mixture of regret, nostalgia, and a
feeling of inevitability. Many Savannahians held fond memories of the train
ride to Tybee and felt regret that a familiar staple of the resort was gone. But
most saw the closing of the Savannah-Tybee branch as the cost of progress.
Few probably could have predicted the effect the loss of reliable rail service
would have on the resort in the decades to come, although this editorial
entitled "DISTANT TYBEE," which appeared in the *Savannah Evening Press*
in February 1933, expressed a prophetic sense of foreboding that the promise
of the auto was not all that it seemed:

> There is a sentimental loneliness in the announcement that the
> Central of Georgia Railroad has discontinued its passenger service
> to Tybee Island. Somehow the beach seems more distant than before
> . . . Many people predicted that a track would not remain on the
> coast. Time and time again sections have been swept away, but the
> railroad passenger service has been a delight to Savannah. Old and
> young by the hundreds have been carried to the far south end in
> summer, and have been brought back at night. Streams have been
> surmounted, draw bridges maintained, and the schedule kept up
> during the summer months.
>   Now we hear that even the omnibus service maintained by the
> railroad has been discontinued. The automobile has robbed the road
> of its patronage; private cars in long lines have been parked along the
> beach, and the railroad could not be expected to maintain its service
> with this competition. We shall miss the summer trains in this despite;
> the whistle and the bell will not be heard any more, and somehow or
> other we feel cut off.

Showers of Flaming Brands

Although the coming of the automobile to the island did much to gradually
change the face of the resort center and the island itself over the course of
several years, Tybee's first major fire dramatically altered the resort district in
mere hours. At 4:00 in the afternoon on July 21, 1931, a small fire began in the
upper story of one of A. F. Solms's Seaside Cottages, which were on the Ocean

Parkway between 16th and 17th Streets. Before the blaze could be brought under control, the fire broke through the roof, where the breeze coming in from the ocean fanned the flames into a roaring inferno. Within minutes several other buildings caught fire as the wind spread the flames from roof to roof. According to the next day's edition of the *Savannah Morning News*, the flames spread in three directions from the Solms Cottage:

> Southward it licked away the buildings as far as the miniature golf course on Seventeenth Street, westward nearly to the tracks of the Central of Georgia Railway, and northward to Sixteenth Street, on which Tybrisa is located.

The Savannah Fire Department was notified soon after the fire began, arriving a half hour later. As there was no water supply available, a pumper truck was run down to the water's edge and ocean water was used to douse the flames. Nearly every man on the island worked to save the buildings and to prevent the spread of the fire. Convicts from the Tybee road camp, firemen, Chatham County and Tybee police, and private citizens all worked to quell the fire and maintain order. A detail of armed soldiers from Fort Screven formed a picket line around the danger zone, patrolling the area and standing guard over what possessions homeowners were able to gather from the burning buildings before they were consumed by flames. Other soldiers from the fort worked with the firefighters, manning two fire wagons requisitioned from the Quartermasters Corps at the base.

After an hour, the buildings in the area where the fire had originated were beyond saving, and all efforts were made to contain the conflagration, which now threatened the entire island, as the roofs of most of the buildings on Tybee were clad with wooden shingles. "Showers of flaming brands" scattered liberally by strong winds ignited small fires on the roofs of cottages as far north as Lovell's Station and Dixon Station. Some buildings were saved by frantic workers who tore away burning shingles and kept streams of water running on the roofs. A great effort was made to prevent the fire from spreading north of 16th Street, as reported in the *Savannah Morning News* the next day:

> On every side men were stationed atop buildings. As fast as they could tear away burning portions of the roofs, other portions would catch, as the wind whipped burning brands in every direction. Izlar's Seabreeze Hotel was threatened many times, the Breakers pavilion caught in a number of places, fire lodged in the south wing of the Hotel Tybee and on the roofs of the cottages on all sides.

It was decided early on by the firefighters that the two story Haar Brothers building, which housed the Ber-Der dining room and store, was a key position in containing the fire, as it was located on the corner of 16th Street and Ocean Parkway, directly across from the Tybrisa Pavilion. It was believed that if the fire claimed the Haar Building, it would be difficult to prevent the blaze from spreading to the pavilion and the resort center. As reported in the *Savannah Morning News*, firefighting crews were relentless in their resolve to save the building and stop the spread of the fire:

> A crew of men on the roof worked heroically . . . with small hose, buckets and hatchets . . . tore away burning shingles . . . and kept the flying embers from gaining a hold. . . . On the sides of the building the fire was kept down by the hoses of the Savannah Fire Department. In saving the Haar building, it is believed that an area as large as that destroyed, represented by the pavilion and the many buildings surrounding it, was saved . . . Had Tybrisa caught the flames would have spread to the Izlar cottages, then to the Seabreeze Hotel; the Breakers and Hotel Tybee pavilion would almost certainly have gone, and cottages all along the beach toward the North End would have been threatened.

The firefighters succeeded in preventing the blaze from spreading north of 16th Street and by 7:30 the fire had been contained and subdued. Although no one was seriously injured in the blaze, the fire destroyed a section of two square blocks, an area roughly centered on Izlar Avenue. Of the 20 buildings that were destroyed, "not a timber was left standing, the places they had occupied being an almost level stretch of smoking ashes."

The fire left over 100 people without shelter. Among the buildings and cottages destroyed were A. F. Solms's Seaside Cottages, where the fire originated; The Perkin's House, also known as the "Shamrock Lodge;" Mrs. Bowen's rooming house, known as the "Waynesboro Tea Room;" the original Carbo House as well as several rental cottages owned by Mrs. J. D. Carbo, E. B. Izlar, and Mrs. Charles B. Cregar; and two private cottages owned by M. Wilinsky and Mrs. Fannie Lasky. Among the businesses destroyed were Joe Whelan's store and Mrs. Harris's Coffee Shop, located in the bottom of the A. F. Solms Cottage. It was later acknowledged that the Tybrisa survived the blaze largely due to the fact that its roof was covered with fire resistant asbestos shingles rather than wood shingles.

As a result of the fire, the Town of Savannah Beach held a special meeting a week later to address the dire need for better fire protection as well as a more adequate water supply.

During the meeting a building ordinance was adopted that provided for the appointment of a building inspector and established a building code that provided guidelines for new construction and for repairs or alterations to existing buildings. The building ordinance contained several provisions that were designed to address existing conditions on Tybee that contributed to the severity of the July 21 fire. For example, the new code prohibited the further use of wooden shingles or other roofing materials not approved by the Fire Underwriters of America. In addition, an ordinance was adopted that created fire limit boundaries for new construction in the resort and boarding house districts. In order to prevent a fire from spreading from one building to another, all new buildings within the boundary area were required to be either of heavy mill or "slow burning construction" or would have to be set back 10 feet from each property line.

Before these improvements could be put in place, however, a second fire, only six weeks later, threatened the resort center once again. On September 2, 1931, fire broke out in one of the resort's four major hotels, the Savannah Beach Hotel, formerly the Lindy Hotel. Located on the corner of Butler Avenue and 15th Street across from the Tybee Station, the two story structure, which housed several businesses on the first floor, was discovered ablaze in the early morning hours. Three companies of soldiers were rushed from Fort Screven to fight the fire and were later joined by two companies of firefighters from Savannah. By the time the firefighters arrived, the hotel was already too far gone to be saved. In an effort to prevent the fire from spreading to the Ocean View Hotel, which was on the opposite corner of the same block, two small frame buildings were razed by Fort Screven soldiers. Due in large part to the early efforts of the soldiers, the fire was quickly contained, the Ocean View Hotel was saved, and the damage from the fire was limited to three-quarters of a block. In all only four buildings were lost to the fire: the Savannah Beach Hotel, which housed Houck's Grocery, Knowles Drugstore, a dentist office, and a barbershop; the Seay Cottage; and two small frame stores, one of which housed Long's Delicatessen. Although wooden roof shingles were not the major factor they were in the July 21 fire, the lack of an adequate water supply was again a major problem in battling the blaze.

Savannah Beach Rebuilds

Despite the loss of a large portion of the boarding house district and a major hotel as a result of the two 1931 fires, Savannah Beach officials remained optimistic for the 1932 season. Earlier in the year, A. F. Solms announced the construction of a new, two story brick hotel along the ocean parkway between 16th and 17th Streets, on the site of his former Seaside Cottages. This substantial 30 room hotel was completed in time for the new season, opening on May 15, 1932. J. D. Carbo, who lost several buildings in the fire, built a new frame 16 room boarding house that same year on the site of the original Carbo House, as well as a small restaurant next door called Carbo's Grill. The new Carbo House and Carbo's Grill served as a catalyst for the early development of 16th Street into Tybee's main commercial corridor during the 1930s and 1940s.

By the mid 1930s, new construction had gradually begun to fill in the lots left vacant by the fire, giving rise to a new commercial center consisting of a mix of concrete block and frame construction (in accordance with the 1931 building code requiring the use of fire-resistant construction in the resort/boarding house district). In an article announcing the opening of the 1937 season, the May 30 edition of the *Savannah Morning News* observed:

> Many new stores, hotels, apartment buildings, and eating places were evidence of greatest optimism for the success of this season at Savannah Beach. Some of the new places have not been quite completed, but almost everything going full tilt gave Tybee a lively aspect.

These new establishments included Wilson's Hotel, a small two story brick building on 16th Street opposite the Carbo House; May's Apartments, a two story brick quadraplex built near the corner of Butler and 16th Streets in 1937; and the Strand Hotel, a two story concrete block/frame building adjacent to Solm's Hotel on the corner of Inlet Avenue and the Strand (*c.* 1935). Several new boarding houses were established during this time as well, including the Beach View Hotel (corner of Butler Avenue and 17th Street) and the Cobb Apartments (corner of 17th Street and Strand), both occupying remodeled, turn-of-the-century summer cottages. A post office and bus station were also established during this time in Tybee's emerging commercial business district, which eventually developed at the intersection of Butler Avenue and 16th Street. The bus station was in a two story frame and concrete block building on the corner of Butler Avenue and 16th Street, and the post office was in a portion of a one story frame and concrete block store at the corner of Butler and Inlet Avenues. One of the first year-round businesses established in the commercial district was Chu's Department Store, which opened in a frame one story building near the corner of 16th Street and the Strand (behind the Haar Building) in 1933. The establishment of Chu's marked the beginning of Tybee's transition into a true year-round community.

Renewal of Oceanfront Resort Center

Although the resort never quite regained the momentum of the 1920s and early 1930s, the Town of Savannah Beach nevertheless remained a popular regional summer destination throughout the rest of the 1930s and the 1940s. In an effort to revitalize the resort, the town launched a beach improvement plan during the late 1930s. Funded in part by a grant from the Federal Works Administration, a concrete seawall and "ocean walkway" was constructed by the Works Progress Administration *c.* 1938–1939 that extended the length of the oceanfront resort area, from 14th to 18th Streets. As part of the improvement plan, the area between 17th and 18th Streets along the Strand was filled in, thus doubling the area of the ocean parkway south of Tybrisa. By this time, the appearance of the oceanfront resort center had changed dramatically from only a few years before. As part of the renewal, the Hotel Tybee Pavilion and the Izlar and Breakers Bathhouses were dismantled, providing a clear view of the beach and ocean from the ocean parkway and walkway in front of Hotel Tybee. A new oceanfront nightclub, called The Brass Rail, was opened during the 1939 season in a remodeled dancing pavilion/restaurant building, formerly part of The Breakers complex. Also during this time, the second floor of the Tybrisa Bathhouse building was remodeled. The open restaurant area was enclosed with windows to create space for a bowling alley, ping pong and pool tables, and a traditional eating area with picnic tables. The 1939 season opened to great fanfare as the resort celebrated a much publicized renewal that led into the new decade.

The Town of Savannah Beach celebrated the beginning of the 1940 season as Tybee's 70th year of operation as a resort (which was technically true, considering regular steamer excursions to the island were offered as early as 1870). The last of Tybee's great hostelries, the Desoto Beach Hotel and Cabana Club, opened on the North End in May of 1940 to much fanfare. Built near the site of Tybee's first resort hotel, the Ocean House, the complex included a clubhouse, two Mediterranean style villas, a cabana court and recreation ground, a pool, and a pavilion and beach shop. The new resort complex was an affiliate of a Savannah-based chain of luxury resort hotels that included the Hotel DeSoto in downtown Savannah, the General Oglethorpe Hotel on Wilmington Island, the Hotel Seminole in Jacksonville, and the Hotel Patten in Chattanooga. At the time of its completion, the Desoto Beach Hotel and Cabana Club was heralded as one of the "finest of its kind on the east coast of the United States."

As a milestone, 1940 may have been more important in the history of the island as it marked the firm establishment of Tybee as a year-round community.

By 1940 the permanent population of Tybee had grown to 636 and more than 600 houses had been built, several of which were built specifically as year-round dwellings. Besides the establishment of a year-round commercial center, other indications of a growing civic environment included the completion of a new $27,000 town hall building on the corner of Butler Avenue and Fourth Street in 1939, the establishment of a public library, and the re-establishment of regular bus service to the island.

During World War II, with shortages and rationing curtailing many recreational pursuits, the resort weathered the anticipated decline in visitation. Like the rest of the nation, the thoughts of Tybee's citizens were focused on the events occurring overseas in Europe and the Pacific. Administered by the Coast Guard, a civilian shore patrol was organized that patrolled the beaches at night between the South End and the light station watching for suspicious activity. Members of Tybee's Power Squadron, a volunteer marine patrol and rescue group, were made auxiliary members of the Coast Guard and were organized to patrol the beaches, creeks, and rivers around Tybee. From atop the Coastal Geodetic and Survey Tower, which was located at the mouth of the Back River (known locally as "The Point"), members of the shore patrol kept watch for surfacing German U-boats, which were ideal for putting enemy agents ashore. During the early years of the war, several U-boat sightings were reported off the coast of Tybee.

The end of World War II brought new prosperity to Tybee. The swift demobilization of the nation's nearly 12 million servicemen following the defeat of the Axis Powers created a nationwide housing shortage. As an inadequate number of private homes were constructed during the Depression and virtually no residential housing was built during the war years, communities throughout the country struggled to provide housing for the nation's fighting men as they re-entered civilian life. Tybee benefited from this trend as there were hundreds of available building lots for purchase on the island, as well as a large stock of second homes that could be utilized as permanent, year-round housing. In February 1946 the *Savannah Morning News* reported "an unprecedented building boom in the building of small homes and remodeling of older residences" on Tybee. That year approximately 50 new houses were built at Savannah Beach for use as year-round housing, in addition to the construction of a new eight unit apartment building on the island. This trend in new construction was attributed to the dramatic growth of Savannah's population and a lack of housing in the city, resulting in many choosing to make their permanent homes on Tybee and commute to Savannah. Many of these new houses were built along Jones and Second Avenue and in the Venetian Terrace Subdivision.

In addition to new construction, the opening of Fort Screven for sale to the public in March 1946 also greatly contributed to the transition of Savannah Beach into a viable year-round community. The residential buildings at Fort Screven were quickly purchased and its warehouses and service-related buildings were converted for residential use. In an effort to accommodate this growing population, two schools were established on the island during this time: the Tybee Public School in 1943 and St. Michael's School, a private Catholic day school, in 1948. Other signs of Savannah Beach's development included the establishment of a second church on the island, the Trinity Methodist Chapel in 1945; the dedication of a new recreation park, called Memorial Park, on Butler Avenue near Town Hall in 1947; and the opening of the Beach Theater in the old Post Theater building at Fort Screven in 1946. By the end of 1940, Tybee had a year-round population of over 1,000.

Chapter Seven

A HONKEY-TONK ECONOMY
AND BEYOND

By the beginning of the 1950s, the Town of Savannah Beach had made the full transition from a seasonal beach resort to a year-round seaside community. This transition brought with it all the growing pains associated with change and expansion. For over 75 years the town operated around the resort, with repairs to infrastructure and other preparations being conducted during the off-season. With a permanent population of over 1,000 at the beginning of the 1950s, the town of Savannah Beach was now also responsible for executing its primary municipal duties on a year-round basis. Although town leaders encouraged and applauded new residential development on the island, no real plans were made to accommodate all the additional growth the town was experiencing. As a result, the town's resources were stretched to the limit while development continued unabated. With the town council's traditional role of supporting and promoting the resort relegated to secondary status, the resort center began to slip into a moral and physical malaise. The inability of the council to keep pace with the demands of a rapidly growing community and its failure to encourage the maintenance and upkeep of resort amenities and infrastructure would have consequences that would later prove dire for the resort and the future success of Savannah Beach.

Main Street Savannah Beach, USA

The opening of the 1950 season marked nearly 60 years of the resort center located at the South End of the island. Originally centered on Hotel Tybee, Tybrisa Pavilion, now the only remaining pavilion on the island, had been the center of resort life since its construction at the end of 16th Street around 1900. The Tybrisa was reopened in 1949 after being rendered unusable following the 1947 hurricane, which caused so much damage on the island. After being repaired and remodeled, the Tybrisa Pavilion, along with the Tybrisa Bathhouse Building, offered resort patrons several new and favorite amusements. According to an article in the May 12, 1949 *Savannah Morning News*, the remodeled pavilion center offered:

> A dance pavilion, skating rink, kiddie boat ride, kiddie chariot ride,
> kiddie auto ride, shooting gallery, a whirling ride, refreshment stands, and
> a coin-in-the slot section featuring everything from undraped beauties of
> 25 years ago to a machine which is supposed to rest weary feet.

The pavilion had been remodeled to house a skating rink in the center, while the outer porches remained a popular place to sit and enjoy the breezes off the ocean.

During the early 1950s, new additions to the resort center included two new U-shaped motel courts, the Waves and Tides Motels, along Butler Avenue across from Hotel Tybee. In addition to these new auto-age hostelries, Tybee Terrace, formerly the American Tourist Court, was established near the Desoto Beach Hotel at the corner of 7th Street and Butler Avenue, adding 16 new concrete block duplexes during the early 1950s.

Perhaps the most noticeable change at Savannah Beach during the early 1950s was the establishment of a traditional commercial district at the intersection of Butler Avenue and 16th Street. This intersection had been the center of the community as early as the 1910s. However, it wasn't until the mid 1950s that the area took on the appearance of a small town commercial district. Reflecting the town's maturation as a year-round community, it was during this time that 16th Street, between Butler Avenue and the Strand, became Tybee's "Main Street." By 1955, a row of one story concrete block storefronts had been established along 16th Street between the bus station and the Carbo House. In 1955 the Beach Drug Company, which opened for business a few years earlier, completed a large, new, one-story stucco building on the north side of 16th Street opposite the bus station. Christies Department Store and Refreshment Stand, on the opposite corner of the Tybrisa Building (16th Street and Strand), was established in the remodeled first floor of the old two story Haar Building (c. 1900s). The street was anchored by T. S. Chu's sprawling one story concrete block department store. The new building, completed c. 1950, became a focal point for the resort, offering exotic imported items from "the Orient" that were ideal for resort patrons and year-round residents alike. By the mid 1950s, Chu's Department Store had expanded, establishing a second ocean side storefront that opened onto the parkway facing the Strand. By the end of the 1950s, most of the area that had been lost to the fire of 1931 had been redeveloped.

The Baby Boom Generation

The post war building boom that had begun on Tybee during the late 1940s continued unabated throughout the early to mid 1950s. Savannah Beach's continued growth as a year-round community during the 1950s resulted in some of the largest residential developments in the island's history. In 1954 a group of Tybee developers announced the construction of the Palm Terrace Subdivision. Located off Highway 80, the new development was situated along Lewis Avenue on a 15 acre track known as "Camp Hammock" (for its proximity to the 4-H Club Camp on the former site of the U.S. Army Diving School). At the time, the Palm Terrace development, which called for the construction of 60 frame, two bedroom, Florida style bungalows, was the largest residential housing project in Tybee's history. A 1955 *Savannah Morning News* advertisement for the development indicated that 34 of the units had been completed by the beginning of the summer season. The headline proclaimed: "$197 NOW starts you on your way to a beautiful year-round home at Savannah Beach just 3 blocks from the ocean." Amenities listed in the advertisement included "city water, hard streets, built in cabinets, and tile baths." Perhaps the most compelling pitch for these simple houses was the terms of sale. With the approval and financing of the Federal Housing Administration, the Palm Terrace Company was able to offer each unit for $6,150 complete, with a total down payment of $498 and a monthly mortgage payment of only $40.41 a month.

In the spring of 1955, the establishment of another residential development on Tybee was announced. Offered by the Tybee Realty Company, the Holiday Park Subdivision offered "well shaded lots on high ground, city water—but no city taxes." Located along the Tybee Road, the development was established on Spanish Hammock, a saltwater hammock just outside the city limits of Tybee. A principal selling point for the development was the fresh water lake in the center of the hammock, as well as an adjacent playground built by the development company. Equally compelling were the terms of sale, in which individual lots were offered for $10 down and $10 a month.

An Aging Resort

By the mid 1950s, despite its growing popularity as a year-round community, Tybee's days as the "Queen of the South Atlantic Resorts" were nearing an end. Although the Town of Savannah Beach remained a popular summer resort, largely as a weekend destination for thousands from south Georgia and coastal Carolina, the resort had begun to show its age, and as a result, had ceased to draw the number of visitors it had only a decade before. Tybee was unable to compete with the newer, more modern middle class beach resorts of south

Florida such as Daytona Beach and Miami Beach, which offered modern, auto-age amenities such as streamlined Art Moderne and Art Deco style hotels, motels, and cabanas as well as high rise luxury hotels along the beach.

In addition to Savannah Beach's dated pavilion center, the resort's problems were compounded by traffic congestion resulting from the two-lane Tybee Road, which was not designed to handle the large volume of weekend traffic now coming to the island during the resort season. By the end of the 1950s, Savannah Beach had a year-round population of 1,300 people. The population would swell to nearly 6,000 during the summer when the cottage owners returned for the resort season. While additional automobile traffic generated by the cottage owners did not present a burden, as these people remained on the island and parked their cars in private drives, the crush of weekend day trippers traveling to Tybee created an enormous problem not only for Savannah Beach, but for those communities along the Tybee Road as well. With the advent of auto tourism, fewer people were staying overnight at Tybee's hotels and boarding houses, preferring instead to spend the day at the beach and drive home. This trend had become firmly entrenched by the 1940s, resulting in frequent traffic jams to and from the island.

The usual 30 minute trip between Savannah and Tybee would often take two hours. Four draw bridges along the route added to the problem by frequently halting traffic and causing hundreds of cars to back up along the highway. Residents of Wilmington Island, which is located along the Tybee Road, were consistently inconvenienced by the weekend traffic to Tybee, having no alternative route to reach their homes and businesses. In addition, the traffic problem had begun to hurt business at the resort, causing many to pine for the "good old days" of the train. By the 1950s, the problem had become acute. With an average of 7,500 day trippers traveling to the island each weekend, Savannah Beach and Chatham County officials realized that something had to be done to alleviate the problem. As early as the mid 1950s, plans were being made to improve the existing Tybee Road as well as provide an alternative route to the island. In 1958, Chatham County officials announced the construction of the "Savannah Beach Expressway," a toll road that would connect downtown Savannah and Tybee. The new route, which was later renamed the "Islands Expressway," would begin at Presidents Street in Savannah, cut across Caustons Bluff, Oatland Island, and Whitmarsh Island, and continue through Wilmington Island where it would tie into the existing Tybee Road just below Bull River. It was hoped that the road would provide the additional benefit of developing the islands along its path. Improvements to the Tybee Road would include replacing the drawbridges at Bull River and Lazaretto Creek and adding a four lane dual highway between Lazaretto Creek and 16th Street. In an effort to alleviate traffic along the Highway 80 section of Wilmington Island, the construction of a bypass between Thunderbolt and Bull River was also to be included in the plans.

Honky Tonk by the Sea

These efforts to improve traffic flow to and from Tybee were too little and too late, as this was only one of several problems facing the resort. By 1960 Savannah Beach had run into hard times, with patronage reaching the lowest level in the history of the resort. As a result, the resort center at Savannah Beach began to decline not only in a physical sense, but in a moral sense as well. The late 1940s marked the last significant remodeling of resort amenities. Eventually boardwalks were neglected and the resort hostelries began to take on an overall shabby appearance. It was about this time that a more rowdy, seedy element began to compete with the general family atmosphere that had always been maintained at the resort. Roadhouses and gambling had always been a part of the resort at Tybee, especially during Prohibition, but these activities had been conducted in back rooms and with discretion. By the mid 1950s Tybee had developed a reputation as a bawdy place, where the limits of the law were stretched and often breached. Doc's Bar and other watering holes such as the Rip Tide and the Novelty Bar were known for their backroom gambling operations, offering craps, slots, and after hour poker games. These same establishments would regularly shirk the blue laws, serving alcohol on Sundays and remaining open until the early hours of the morning. These illegal activities were well known by all, even law enforcement, who for years looked the other way. Tybee's pavilion center was also a place where a "john" could find "female companionship" after hours. The Carbo House on 16th Street operated as a well known brothel during this time. Prostitutes with such colorful names as "Shopping Bag Betty, Mattress Mary, and Kandy Kane," were well known along the boardwalk. Like Coney Island and other aged, turn of the century resorts struggling to attract commerce, some of Tybee's merchants began to cater to the lowest common denominator.

The *Savannah Morning News*, which had long been a champion of the resort, openly denounced the avarice and general vice that had become prevalent on Tybee in an editorial written by Joseph E. Lambright on September 3, 1957. Lambright began his piece, entitled "Shameful Conditions Demand Action," bluntly declaring that "Chatham County should be thoroughly ashamed of

Savannah Beach." Lambright continued to chastise the physical and moral deterioration of the resort on Tybee, calling for an end to what he referred to as Savannah Beach's "honky-tonk economy:"

> Endowed by nature with assets that could make it one of the best, cleanest and most attractive resorts along the South Atlantic coast, Tybee has instead permitted itself to be exploited in the wrong way, so that its reputation throughout our state is based on its infamy, rather than its fame.
>
> There is no valid reason for Tybee's continued dependence on what can only be termed a honky-tonk economy. The greater Savannah area, of which Savannah Beach is a part, has long ago outgrown this sort of thing. . . . To those who argue that traffickers in alcohol, gambling, disregard of the Sabbath, and the assorted accompanying evils are entitled to make a living at it, we can only ask: Why? It is illegal. It contributes nothing new to our community. We don't need it. And we should not tolerate it.

Lambright concluded his list of vices perpetrated on Tybee with the corrupting influence Savannah Beach was having on the youth of Savannah. As it had been with the flappers of the Roaring Twenties, Hotel Tybee was again "the scene of the crime" 30 years later, but this time the culprit was rock and roll and "the twist" rather than up-tempo jazz and the "Charleston:"

> The spectacle of reveling teen-agers, some scarcely of the age of puberty, assembled into a bacchanalian maelstrom of frantic worship at the altar of rock'n'roll on the evening of the Lord's Day, as was the case Labor Day eve at the Hotel Tybee, is at best disgusting.

Despite public admonishment by the local press during the late 1950s, these events at Savannah Beach continued unabated for several years until 1963, when an article in the *Atlanta Constitution* brought state-wide attention to Tybee. The article declared that Tybee was "as wide open as Phenix City, Alabama ever was," drawing an unflattering comparison of Savannah Beach with a town that had gained national notoriety during the early 1960s as a "community of vice and corruption." The paper maintained that whisky was sold to underage patrons and that

> gambling goes on in barrooms and some gambling is done on the bar. At least three night spots have gambling rooms in the back where players lose money in black jack and at the crap tables.

As a result of this article, Chatham County officials were under considerable political pressure from the governor's office to address the situation. On April 17, 1963, Chatham County sheriff Carl Griffin declared a county-wide ban on underage drinking and gambling, which was to take effect on May 1 that year. The following day, the *Savannah Morning News* covered the story under the headline "Sheriff Declares War on Chatham Gambling: Beach Told Machines Must Go." In a separate article published the same day, William H. "Willie" Harr, owner of the Brass Rail, said of the ban on gambling machines:

> I guess it will hurt business all right, if they do have to come down . . . This is a resort. People come down here to have a little fun. If they are going to run it like a church, I don't think they'll have many people down here.

Unlike past attempts to quell illicit activities on the island, the ban was enforced, putting an end to Tybee's days as a seaside casino. In addition, new county regulations were passed prohibiting underage persons from entering bars or other places where alcohol is served.

The Modern Auto-Age Resort

At the same time that Savannah Beach was cleaning up its act, the town's civic leaders were busy implementing plans to revive Tybee as a regional resort destination. Officials were hopeful that the completion of the new Islands Expressway, which would provide a direct link between downtown Savannah and Tybee, would serve as a much needed catalyst for Savannah Beach's renewal. The new route, as well as improvements to the Tybee Road, would alleviate traffic congestion to and from Tybee, providing a more enjoyable experience for resort patrons. In addition, civic leaders anticipated a steady flow of out-of-state traffic from two newly completed interstate highways, I-16 and I-95, both of which fed directly into downtown Savannah. The opening of the expressway in 1964 was heralded as a new beginning for Savannah Beach and the outlying islands of Chatham County.

Influenced in part by the urban renewal movement of the late 1950s and early 1960s, Tybee endured its own version of this ill-conceived national program. In an effort to modernize the resort center to reflect the auto age amenities of the newer resorts, especially the east coast beach towns of Florida, several plans were made that would eventually bring a dramatic change to the physical appearance of the island.

Unfortunately, Hotel Tybee was the first victim of urban renewal at Savannah Beach. Perhaps the most enduring landmark of Tybee's golden era as a resort, Hotel Tybee was the very essence of late-period Victorian splendor, evoking the days of train travel, dance cards, and bath house bathing. But like other plush, turn-of-the century resort hotels across the nation, Hotel Tybee was now seen as an outdated "queen dowager," admittedly grand and dignified, but too fussy and formal for the modern auto tourist. As a result, the north wing of Hotel Tybee was converted into a 22-room motel in 1958. In 1961, plans were announced that called for the demolition of the central, three-and-half story, main mass of the hotel. According to the plans, which were announced in the January 19, 1961 *Savannah Morning News* under the headline "Tybee Hotel Gets Ready for Tunnel," the main center section would be demolished in order to create a private road from Butler Avenue to the beach. In addition, the remaining south wing would be converted into a second 22-room motel unit. Although the first phase of the hotel's redevelopment was carried out with the demolition of the main hotel structure on February 1 of that year, the second phase of converting the south wing into a motel was never accomplished. Eventually, the south wing was demolished as well, and several small, one and two story motels were erected on the property along 14th Street and the oceanfront by the early 1970s. These included the Verandah Motel (oceanfront at Strand and 15th Street), the Sands Motel (14th Street and Strand), and Days Inn, located along Butler Avenue at the corner of 14th Street. Built in 1970 by Cecil Day, an Atlanta developer, Days Inn at Tybee was the first unit of what later became the Days Inn hotel and motel chain.

End of an Era

In 1964 plans were announced that called for the long overdue revitalization of the oceanfront resort center. Perhaps as a consequence of the 1963 ban on gambling, W. H. Haar, who had owned and operated businesses on Tybee since the 1930s, sold the bulk of his oceanfront property to E. C. Bobo, a Savannah Beach businessman, who planned to develop the property as an entertainment center along the boardwalk. Centered on the Tybrisa Pavilion, Tybee's last major resort attraction, the real estate deal included more than half of the two block area bounded by 15th and 16th Streets, representing the core of the resort's historic boardwalk center. According to the *Savannah Morning News* of January 3, 1964, the transaction included the following properties:

> The Brass Rail building, the amusement area fronting the boardwalk, the Fascination Bingo building, Tybrisa Building which comprises the bath houses, the Rip Tide Bar, bowling alley, refreshment stands adjoining the strand, the S&S Restaurant on 16th Street, and Tybrisa Pavilion.

As another article in the *Savannah Morning News* pointed out, the property consisted of several acres with "aging improvements," including the site of the Sea Breeze Hotel (*c.* 1910s), which was razed after a fire gutted the building in 1963.

Bobo's plans included the rehabilitation of the Tybrisa Pavilion and the Tybrisa Bathhouse Building, as well as the construction of a new, modern bath house along Atlantic Avenue. The entertainment area, which was to be called "Tybeeland," was planned as a more family-oriented establishment.

In addition to the planned revitalization of the Tybrisa property, the Savannah Beach Town Council resolved that same year to investigate the possibility of purchasing the Tybee Motel (formerly Hotel Tybee) or the Desoto Beach Hotel, which had been closed since 1962, for use as a convention center. The town council also announced plans for the construction of a new municipal fishing pier at the end of 1st Street to replace the old pier located at the end of the Tybrisa pavilion that was washed away during a storm in 1963.

As fate would have it, only one of these plans, the new fishing pier, came to fruition. Although the Desoto Beach Hotel would eventually reopen and serve the island for several more decades, plans for the revitalization of the oceanfront resort center tragically came to an end after a suspicious fire in 1967 that destroyed the Tybrisa Pavilion and over a block of Tybee's remaining historic oceanfront resort amenities.

As reported the following morning, May 17, in the *Savannah Morning News*, the fire, which was discovered about 9:45 p.m., raged out of control for several hours, destroying the Tybrisa Pavilion, the two story Tybrisa Building—which contained the Riptide Bar and Lounge, a dance hall, and bowling alley—two concession stands, and the Funhouse Arcade, as well as the boardwalks and other small buildings along the oceanfront. According to the article, "smoke towered between 150–200 feet in the air and could be seen in Savannah, almost 20 miles away."

Christy's, a concession store on the 16th Street strand directly across from the Tybrisa Building and pavilion, was also gutted by the fire. Firemen fought to contain the blaze in order to save the T. S. Chu & Co. Variety Store, which was located on 16th Street in back of Christy's. Ironically, the building that

Christy's occupied, the old Haar Building (*c.* 1900s), was the focal point in 1931 when firemen fought to save the building in an effort to prevent the spread of fire beyond 16th Street to the Tybrisa Building.

In a separate article that same morning, the *Savannah Morning News* reported that Savannah Beach Police were holding a 16-year-old boy, an employee of the pavilion, on suspicion of arson. Although the boy admitted to starting the fire because he had not been paid his wages, the ultimate fate of the property appears to lie in the contentious events that surrounded its sale and ownership in the years before the fire. Despite the lease-purchase agreement that W. H. Haar entered into with E. C. Bobo and Tybeeland Inc., Haar's wife Evelyn challenged the validity of the contract following her husband's death later that year. The court eventually ruled in favor of Evelyn Haar and the property was returned to her control in 1966. Haar sold the property to Pavilion Inc. later that same year. As a result of the lawsuit, the Tybrisa property, the heart of Tybee's oceanfront resort area, sat vacant and unattended from 1963 to 1967, depriving Tybee of a major resort attraction for four years. Already deteriorated when it was closed in 1963, there is no doubt that the additional years of neglect did little to improve the public perception of Tybee's aged resort center, which by this time was seen as beyond repair.

This sentiment is vividly revealed in an editorial in the *Savannah Morning News* on the morning after the fire. Written by Assistant City Editor Archie Whitfield, the editorial, rather than memorializing the loss of the old pavilion center, appears to portray the disaster as a merciful act of fate. Entitled "Historical Buildings Ravaged," the editorial implies that the fire acted as a force of urban renewal:

> Fire dramatically overtook time and nature's other less violent elements when it stepped in Tuesday night to wipe out the old Tybrisa Pavilion and Tybrisa Building at Savannah Beach. . . . The Tybrisa structures had been the focal point of entertainment and recreation for thousands of Savannahians, many of whom considered them deteriorating symbols of "the good old days."

Constantly referring to the pavilion as "old," "shabby," and "deteriorated" throughout the piece, it is clear that the paper's editorial staff thought the structures were beyond rehabilitating. It is telling that the same newspaper that heralded E. C. Bobo and Tybeeland's plans to renovate the property only three years earlier now openly applauded the destruction of Tybee's historic oceanfront boardwalk area as an inevitable occurrence. There is little doubt that support for this position came with the assumption that the site would be redeveloped and Tybrisa would be replaced with new, modern resort amenities that would help revive Savannah Beach's flagging tourism industry. An article that appeared the following week echoed this sentiment: "the building may not be replaced, but one old-timer whose memory pre-dates the 20th century believes that the recent fire 'could be the start of a happy new era that we need very badly at Tybee.'"

Unfortunately, this happy new era was not to be realized in the twentieth century. The assumption that a developer would seize the opportunity to replace the Tybrisa turned out to be overly optimistic and as a result, the property sat vacant for the remainder of the 1960s. In 1971 the Savannah Beach Town Council purchased the property after a buyer could not be found, and in 1973, the council revealed plans to redevelop the oceanfront property into a boardwalk mall area with restaurants, shops, and an amusement center. These plans never came to fruition.

The destruction of the Tybrisa and the failure to redevelop the site during the decades that followed left Savannah Beach without a major resort attraction. As a result, Tybee no longer attracted the throngs of out-of-town visitors it had during its heyday. Savannah Beach began a gradual, decades-long decline into a sleepy little beach town, largely overlooked as a regional seaside resort destination. Despite these realities, however, some aspects of island life remained unchanged throughout the 1970s, 1980s, and 1990s. Tybee Island still had its first and best attraction—its miles of "white sand beaches"—and Savannah Beach continued to be a popular weekend beach destination for Savannahians and the nearby counties of South Georgia. As in decades past, Tybee's summer cottage owners continued to return each season to their family retreats to spend the summer.

Ironically, as Savannah Beach declined as a seaside resort, the town continued to grow as a year-round community. In 1970 Savannah Beach had a population of 1,800. By 1980 the population had grown to 2,200, an increase of nearly 20 percent. During this period, the year-round housing built on the island began to reflect more closely the architecture of suburban Savannah rather than the frame Tybee beach cottages of the 1920s and 1930s. In 1971 the Chu family established the first convenience store on the island at the corner of Highway 80 and Jones Avenue. In addition, new low-rise motels and condominiums were gradually built where the heart of the resort had once been. Unable to find an investor to develop the site as a municipal resort attraction, the Savannah Beach Town Council eventually sold the

Tybrisa property to a real estate developer. As a result, Tybee's first large scale condominiums, Tybee Ocean Villas, were built in 1981. Located between 15th and 16th Streets, the new three story buildings formed an unwelcoming, private "residential wall" along the oceanfront Strand area. The privatization of Tybee's historic oceanfront resort center set an unfortunate and avoidable precedent. Once touted as "Georgia's Playground," Tybee's accessibility to the middle class would increasingly be undermined in the decades to come.

Tybee Remembers its Past

As Savannah Beach struggled to create a new, more modern, auto-age resort during the 1960s, the community acknowledged its storied past through the establishment of two new heritage projects. Sponsored by the Savannah Beach Chamber of Commerce, eight Georgia historical markers were erected in 1958 at several historic sites on Tybee and nearby Cockspur Island. The handsome bronze markers highlighted the rich military and maritime heritage of the area, concentrating mostly on the Colonial and Civil War periods. On Tybee, markers were erected for the Lazaretto, the Federal Batteries, Fort Screven, and Tybee Lighthouse. On Cockspur Island, which was by this time a unit of the National Park Service, markers were erected for Fort Pulaski, John Wesley, and the Waving Girl. Later that same year the chamber of commerce announced plans to establish a history museum in Battery Garland (*c.* 1899), one of the six reinforced-concrete coast artillery batteries that made up Fort Screven. Directly across from the Tybee Lighthouse, the location of the new museum was ideal. Completed in 1961, the Tybee Museum featured several collections of historical items, documents, dioramas, pictures, and relics that chronicled the different periods of the island's history, ranging from the Guale Indians through "Spanish pirates, Oglethorpe, the Revolutionary War, the Civil War, old Tybee days and up to modern times." The museum proved very popular with tourists, attracting over 8,000 visitors in its first summer. Both the marker project and the museum were a concerted effort by the Savannah Beach Chamber of Commerce to tap into the island's heritage tourism potential by associating the history of Tybee Island with Fort Pulaski National Monument. It was also hoped that the Tybee Museum would add an additional attraction to aid in the effort to make Savannah Beach a year-round resort.

In 1986, Tybee gained its greatest modern tourist attraction when the Tybee Museum Society assumed responsibility for the Tybee Lighthouse from the U.S. Coast Guard, which had relocated to a new base of operations at Station Tybee on Cockspur Island. The Tybee Museum Society, which was formed in 1976 to assume operation of the Tybee Museum from the city, changed its name to the Tybee Island Historical Society in 1986 to reflect its expanded role as steward of both the museum and lighthouse. Although the Tybee Lighthouse remained an operating aid to navigation, the Tybee Island Historical Society, through a lease with the U.S. Coast Guard, was now responsible for maintenance of the lighthouse itself and the numerous support buildings that made up the light station. Responsibility for the light station allowed the historical society to give tours of the lighthouse and support buildings for the first time. The lighthouse rapidly became Tybee's most popular attraction, commanding over 65,000 visitors a year. In 1994 the Tybee Island Historical Society was fortunate to engage the services of one of the nation's premier lighthouse conservators, Cullen Chambers, who assumed the position of executive director of the Tybee Island Historical Society. Although Chambers had contributed to the preservation of several lighthouses along the east coast, he was best known for his work in Key West and St. Augustine. In addition to his expertise during the ambitious restoration of the light station during the early 2000s, Chambers's leadership would prove to be a pivotal factor in the struggle to preserve Tybee's historic neighborhoods and cottages in the years to come.

Truck Stop by the Sea

Apart from the construction of a few new hotels and two new condominium projects on the island's North Side (facing the Savannah River), very little development occurred on Tybee throughout the 1980s and the early 1990s. As if determined to turn its back on its own resort past, the town council changed the name of the community from the Town of Savannah Beach back to Tybee Island during the early 1980s. By the 1990s, Tybee's oceanfront and commercial area had become somewhat threadbare and neglected. Apart from the "Kiddie Fair," a small amusement center with a Ferris Wheel and rides established *c.* 1960 as "Eastin's Ride Center," there was practically no family entertainment along 16th Street. Other then Chu's and Christie's Department Stores, Tybee's "main street" was mostly populated by seedy bars and a few small restaurants. In addition, most of Tybee's boarding houses had become derelict and rundown. Many of these buildings had been converted into low-rent, year-round apartments that attracted a somewhat transient population. Although Tybee's residential and summer cottage owners remained good stewards, maintaining their cottages and property, what remained of the resort area had become, to most people, a blight on the island. By this time many had forgotten or were unaware of Tybee's grand past as the Queen of the South

Atlantic Resorts. The perception of most Savannahians was that Tybee was a rundown backwater offering little more than bars and beach, earning such derogatory (yet colorful) nicknames as "Mayberry on Acid," "Truck Stop by the Sea," and "Red Neck Riviera."

Despite the attitudes of Savannahians, many year-round residents were proud of the laid back atmosphere and cherished their island community. In their view, Tybee was a "state of mind," offering an inexpensive, beautiful seaside living environment. Out-of-town visitors to Tybee would often be heard to comment on its "quirky" mix of old and new, its colorful variety of people, and its open, easily accessible public beach. The fact that Tybee had not been as overdeveloped as most barrier islands outside of Georgia was another point often heard. Despite its dilapidated oceanfront area and the lack of a major resort attraction, Tybee offered a diversity and charm not found in other coastal resort communities. By 1990 the City of Tybee Island, which now encompassed practically the entire island, had a population of 2,800 residents.

Tybee Rediscovered

The announcement that Atlanta would be the host city of the 1996 Centennial Summer Olympic Games was a singular event that dramatically changed Tybee's fortunes. In anticipation of the international visitors that would be coming to Atlanta as well as to several other cities throughout the state, plans were made to spruce up downtowns and to build or improve existing facilities in the cities and towns hosting events. Tybee was initially chosen as the host site for the beach volleyball competition, as well as a support site for the sailing competition, which was headquartered at the former General Oglethorpe Hotel (later the Sheraton Resort) on Wilmington Island. The coming of the Olympics to Georgia was the catalyst needed to spur the Chatham County Board of Commissioners to commit to the long talked about construction of a new pier on the original site of the Tybrisa. The new Tybee Pier, which featured a large picnic pavilion area and a fishing pier that extended out into the Atlantic, was completed and opened in the spring of 1996, just prior to the start of the Olympics. Although Tybee ended up losing the opportunity to host the volleyball competition, thousands of visitors descended on Savannah and the surrounding area to view the sailing events. Interest in Savannah, fueled by its lovely squares, the elegant nineteenth-century architecture of its Landmark Historic District, and the international notoriety gained through "The Book"—John Berendt's *Midnight in the Garden of Good and Evil*—led to an intense media scrutiny of all places associated with the city. As a result, Tybee was rediscovered.

The rapid redevelopment of Tybee Island began even before the first piling of the new pavilion was driven into the sand. Fueled in part by an accelerating national trend toward coastal development, the combination of relatively inexpensive seaside real estate and the distinction of being an Olympic host site made Tybee a perfect new candidate for development. While this investment in Tybee was good news for the community as a whole, it was a devastating blow for Tybee's preservation community. In 1995 alone, 13 historic boarding houses were demolished for their oceanfront lots by developers planning to erect condos in their place. This action squelched efforts by the Tybee Island Historical Society to list what remained of the historic oceanfront resort area on the National Register of Historic Places. Demolition of historic resources in the boarding house district continued over the next several seasons, resulting in the demolition of the four-unit Cobb Apartments in 1997, the dismantling of the Tybee Island Amusement Center in 1998 (the "Kiddie Fair" on 16th Street) to make way for the construction of a new Super 8 Motel, and the wholesale demolition of five boarding houses along 17th Terrace in 1999. With the demolition of the old Solms Hotel in 2002 and the construction of yet another condo in its place, a row of nondescript three story condominium buildings extended the length of the oceanfront strand from Izlar Avenue to 18th Street.

Although this rash of demolition did not go unnoticed, the most contentious and controversial loss during this time was the old Mediterranean villa–style Desoto Beach Hotel in 1999. Built in 1940, the Desoto Beach Hotel and Cabana Club was the last of Tybee's major historic resort hostelries. The villa resort complex had the distinction of being one of three host sites for the 1947 International Monetary Conference. Based in Savannah, the conference was the inaugural meeting of the international organization now known as the World Bank. Lead by Cullen Chambers and the Tybee Island Historical Society, local preservationists appealed to city council to grant a stay of demolition in an effort to reach a compromise with the developer in order to save the building. Despite these efforts, and vocal public opposition, the historic hotel was demolished and a massive, oversized complex was built in its place.

Although the loss of the Desoto was unfortunate, the publicity surrounding the event increased public awareness and interest in what remained of Tybee's historic resources, resulting in the restoration of several summer cottages and a renewed appreciation of Tybee's classic coastal resort architecture. Tybee residents were no longer willing to accept the unchecked condo development that had dominated the island since 1995. In 1999 the city council imposed a year-long moratorium on new construction in order to develop a plan to more efficiently control new growth. Through the leadership of the Tybee Island Historical Society, several preservation projects were completed during this time, including the listing of the Strand Cottages and the Back River Historic Districts on the National Register of Historic Places in 1999, the rescue of the *c.* 1925 Post Theater in 2002 (which the historical society purchased jointly with the city) and the completion of an island-wide inventory of Tybee's historic resources in 2003.

Although the Tybee Island Historical Society's efforts were indeed a central force in the preservation of the island's historic resort architecture, its most enduring legacy to date is undoubtedly its conservation work regarding its principal mission—the stewardship of the Tybee Light Station. After years of planning and fundraising, Cullen Chambers and the Tybee Island Historical Society began a monumental four phase restoration of the light station in 1999. Acknowledged as one of the most intact light stations in the nation, Tybee Light Station boasts five historic support buildings arranged in a garrison plan (dating back to Union occupation from 1861–1867). When completed, the Lighthouse (*c.* 1773/1867), the Head Keepers Cottage (*c.* 1881), the First Assistant Keepers Cottage (*c.* 1885), and the Second Assistant Keepers Cottage (*c.* 1862) would all be restored to their *c.* 1900 appearance. Through the considerable expertise of Chambers, the multi-million dollar restoration of the Lighthouse and Head Keepers Cottage were completed by 2003, with both projects receiving preservation awards of excellence from the National Trust for Historic Preservation and the Historic Preservation Division of the Georgia Department of Natural Resources. In 2004 the Tybee Island Historical Society, through the impressive demonstration of its stewardship of the historic resources under its care, earned the distinction of being the first recipient of the Lighthouse Transfer Program, a program of the Department of Interior in which ownership of the nation's historic lighthouses are transferred to able organizations or entities who are entrusted with their care and maintenance.

Today Tybee Island is perhaps as popular as it ever was during its heyday. In addition to the beaches, lighthouse, and pavilion, Tybee now offers visitors and residents a variety of restaurants, shops, and nightlife. From the modern million-dollar oceanfront retreat to a turn-of-the-century one room cottage, the range and variety of rental and housing options on the island is as varied as its eclectic mix of residents. New or old, large or quaint, Tybee's historic frame beach cottages and mid-century concrete block houses complement the new oceanfront condos, hotels, and residences, providing accommodations to fit most any preference. With the construction of the Tybee Pier, the island appears to have come full circle, and is perhaps finally beginning "a happy new era" that has eluded the community for so long.

TYBEE'S UNIQUE COASTAL RESORT ARCHITECTURE

One of Tybee's most enduring legacies as a summer resort is the unique character of its vernacular, coastal resort architecture. Built during the island's heyday as a summer resort (roughly 1880–1950), Tybee's private summer cottages were designed to take advantage of, and be prepared for, the forces of nature typical of Tybee and other similar low lying coastal areas. The architectural characteristics of the Tybee summer cottage are based on a simple yet unique design that affords the occupants a "comfortable advantage" during the hot summer months while employing a functionality that adapts well to the coastal environment for which they were designed.

Characteristics of Tybee's Summer Cottages

The design of Tybee's cottages is principally derived from French, British, and Spanish colonial architectural traditions. Like the eighteenth and nineteenth century cottages of the Caribbean and the Mississippi delta, Tybee's cottages draw heavily on French Colonial innovations designed to minimize the severity of a humid climate. As Tybee's builders undoubtedly understood, the raised Creole houses of the Mississippi delta, which they principally based their designs on, were ideal for the hot, humid climate of coastal Georgia.

Like the Creole house, the raised design of Tybee cottages not only protected the main living quarters from rising tides but also improved air circulation, helping to cool the home. Lattice work surrounding the ground level (a characteristic of many Tybee cottages) allowed for enhanced air flow under the open raised structure, producing a drying effect that helped deter rotting of the buildings' trussed piers and lower level framing.

The high pitch of the roof, another hallmark of French Colonial architecture, is another design aspect intended to maximize the cool breezes coming off the ocean. This high pitch in conjunction with vents along the porch overhang and the top of the roof allowed rising hot air to escape, causing a cooling updraft.

Tybee cottages typically feature deep, recessed wraparound porches that often extend around three or more sides. This is particularly true of the older cottages on the South End along the Back River, which typically feature recessed porches that wrap around all four sides. The deep porches shade the walls of the building and keep the rooms cool while open windows, doors, and interior transoms allow cool ocean breezes to flow through the house. As with the Creole houses, Tybee porches were utilized as an extension of the main living quarters in which occupants would eat or socialize, and often sleep on hot summer nights. The humidity, heat, and direction of the breeze determined the areas of the building that would be utilized at any given time. Also like the Creole cottage, the wraparound porch of the Tybee cottage and the floor plan are interconnected. There are no interior passage halls in Creole cottages. Rather, the gallery served as passageways and stair halls. Similarly, the rooms of Tybee cottages, especially the bedrooms, often open onto the porch as well as interior rooms. Although there are a variety of floor plans, many Tybee cottages display a variation of a common plan found in the raised cottages of the Mississippi Delta region in which smaller private rooms are situated around a large central, common room.

Another characteristic that differentiates Tybee's summer cottages from other regional coastal resort architecture is the material used in its construction. Tybee cottages were almost exclusively built of heart pine. Heart pine framing and interior walls, ceilings, and floors provided a lightweight material that was inexpensive and relatively easy to transport. The interior surfaces of Tybee cottages were generally left unpainted, and clear shellac was applied to protect the wood. Originally the roofs were covered with wood shingles, a practice prohibited by a town ordinance following the great fire of 1931. Traditionally, the exterior clapboards of Tybee cottages were painted white, while the wood shutters, window and door frames, porch railings, and other trim were painted a dark "cottage green."

In addition to the beauty of its natural finish, the use of pine in the construction of Tybee cottages provided many practical advantages. Pine is filled with sap that deters termites. It allows the cottage to move and give way to strong winds associated with the frequent summer storms and the occasional hurricanes common to coastal areas. In a sense, pine framing allows a building to bend, not break. A more rigid structure might prove too resistant to high winds and collapse during severe storms or hurricanes.

Summer Cottage Development on Tybee

From the very beginning of the resort, summer cottages were built along the oceanfront and the Back River in close proximity to the hotels and pavilions of the resort center. By the mid twentieth century these distinct square two story frame cottages with their characteristic high pitched hip roofs and deep, recessed wraparound porches dotted every corner of the island. Tybee's summer cottages were built as casual retreats for communal living with family and friends. Families from Savannah and throughout the region would often return each year to spend the season at their summer cottage, a tradition that would often span several generations.

The Strand and Back River neighborhoods, which represent the oldest and most substantial concentration of resort cottages remaining on Tybee, are summer resort settlements that developed between 1895 and 1920 as a direct result of the construction of the Savannah-Tybee Railroad in 1887 and the construction of Hotel Tybee on the South End of the island in 1891.

The Strand

The area sandwiched between Tybee's first major hotels, Hotel Tybee and the Ocean House, is the location of the original Strand. These lots were desirable due to their oceanfront locations and their close proximity to the two main resort centers. In addition, the railroad had five stops along Main Street (later Butler Avenue) that made these lots easily accessible. The Strand district was one of the first areas of the island to build up as a direct result of these factors.

Although the earliest construction in the Strand district began with the completion of the Ocean House in 1876 and the subsequent development that built up around it, very little of this section was left by the turn of the century. Few buildings on the island survived the devastating hurricanes of 1881, 1893, and 1898. In addition, fires frequently claimed both lives and wooden structures.

Located between 12th and 14th Streets, the oldest buildings remaining in the Strand district are a row of private summer cottages next to Hotel Tybee known as the "Strand Cottages." Built between 1895 and 1920, each cottage was built in the center of a full oceanfront lot that extended from Butler Avenue to the beach. As the row took shape, a common landscape theme was adopted by each subsequent addition. All cottages were built at a substantial setback from the dunes, which provided a grassy expanse (or strand) with wax myrtle, various palmetto trees, mature oaks, and sand dunes between the homes and the beach. A walkway passed in front of the steps of each cottage, connecting the settlement with the resort at Hotel Tybee. This arrangement afforded the property owners a spacious and private setting with a somewhat communal aspect when desired. In addition, each cottage had a bridle path to the beach that ran off the walkway.

The Strand Cottages are rectangular, with hip roofs with overhanging eaves, recessed wraparound porches, and braced frame construction with mortise-and-tenon joinery. Most of the cottages are raised a half story on trussed wooden piers. Servant's quarters and changing rooms (for ocean bathing) were on the ground or "basement" level with the main living quarters on the raised level. The main quarters of most examples appear to be a variation of the bungalow floor plan, although some have Georgian-derived floor plans as well (a central hallway with two equal sized rooms on each side). Strand cottages are generally more ornate than South End/Back River cottages. Many feature floor length windows, French doors, stained glass windows, transom and sidelight door surrounds, pressed metal shingles, roof finials, bay windows, and polygonal corner porches.

The Tybee Island Strand Cottages Historic District, listed on the National Register of Historic Places in 1999, is recognized by the Department of Interior as "an excellent collection of summer resort cottages . . . unique to Georgia due to their coastal resort features" and as "the only intact historic cottages remaining on the island associated with the American coastal resort movement along the Atlantic Ocean and with the development of Hotel Tybee."

The Back River

Established at the same time as the Strand, the Back River district is an early twentieth century concentration of beach resort cottages at the mouth of and along the length of the Back River at Tybee's South End. While many summer cottages were built along the oceanfront near the resort hotels, bath houses, and pavilions, this area was developed as a more secluded alternative to the frenetic bustle of the resort. Most of the cottages were built for families from Savannah.

The most intact group of cottages offering the most unadulterated portrayal of the architectural and landscape characteristics of the district are between Inlet Avenue and the mouth of the Back River. This row of cottages, sometimes referred to as "Colony Row," was built between 1900 and 1909. Each cottage is situated in the center of a one-and-a-half acre lot facing the river.

Most of these cottages, referred to as South End/Back River Cottages, are large, two-story, square, hip roof buildings with recessed, double wraparound porches with floor length windows and French doors. Originally, the porches extended around all four sides of the building. The main living quarters are on the upper floor with the dining room and other service-oriented facilities on the lower floor. Unlike the Strand Cottages, servant quarters and bathhouses were located in separate buildings in back of the main house.

Sam Varnedoe, a Tybee native whose family moved to the island in 1909, described what the Back River area looked like in his short history, "Memoir of Tybee Island: 1909–1988." In reference to the South End/Back River Cottages of Colony Row, Varnedoe recalled that "all of the row of cottages were built facing the ocean or inlet" and that the cottages "must have been built by the same architect or contractor, because they were all built square-shaped with the same type roof and a servants house on the back of each cottage." According to Varnedoe, a small house was situated in the back of every cottage to house a barrel of oil for lighting, and chicken yards were also common. As was the practice with many turn-of-the-century river and beach resort developments, all the cottages were connected by wood boardwalks. Originally, a boardwalk ran the length of the bluff in front of the cottages, extending from the Point to Inlet Station, where the Central of Georgia turnstile was located.

The Tybee Back River Historic District, listed on the National Register of Historic Places in 1999, is recognized by the Department of Interior as the largest concentration (historically or today) of coastal resort cottages in Georgia, representing the oldest and best examples of summer cottages associated with the American coastal resort movement in Georgia.

The Raised Tybee Cottage

The beach houses that have come to be known as Raised Tybee Cottages were first introduced during Tybee's golden era as a coastal summer resort. Built between the early 1920s and the late 1940s, the Raised Tybee Cottage retains several design elements of the earlier cottages built on the island while providing a new functionality that lent itself more effectively to the trends brought on by the new resorts of the Roaring Twenties.

The Raised Tybee Cottage is characterized as a frame, generally square, two story beach house in which the main living quarters are situated on the raised level and servants quarters, changing rooms, and automobile stalls are located on the ground level. The main living quarters are generally raised on trussed wood piers, with the ground level enclosed with wood lattice in which lattice garage doors face side streets or lanes. Most examples have hip roofs, which are often covered with pressed metal shingles, and recessed wraparound porches. Early Raised Tybee Cottages feature a casual, communal open plan in which the entrance opens into a large common room or parlor that is flanked on both sides by several smaller rooms. Bedrooms are usually located along the side porch, with service oriented rooms (kitchen, bathroom, etc.) on the opposite side of the parlor. The parlor is generally quite large and serves several functions, often doubling as a casual dining area. Raised Tybee Cottages are generally smaller than their predecessors in order to take advantage of smaller building lots.

The completion of the Tybee Road in 1923 ushered in a golden era for Tybee. As a result of the island's increased accessibility, the resorts flourished and Tybee entered an unparalleled building boom. It was during this time that Cab Calloway, Bob Crosby, and other Big Band personalities performed at Tybee's dancing pavilions and the island was arguably the most popular resort on the south Atlantic coast. Rows of boarding houses were built and numerous small hotels were established during this time to accommodate the crush of people visiting the island. It was during this time that the classic Raised Tybee Cottage was first introduced.

The opening of the Tybee Road spurred a dramatic increase in the demand for oceanfront property, causing development and construction practices in the Strand district to change dramatically. Because the island was more accessible than ever before, more people were interested in beach cottages. Instead of one large cottage being built in the center of an original oceanfront lot, the lots were subdivided and many smaller cottages were built. The small size of the lots required a different type of cottage than those built on the island in previous years, thus providing the inspiration for the new cottages.

Whether or not it was the intention of Tybee's cottage builders of the 1920s and 1930s, the new cottages in many ways appeared to be a combination of the Strand and South End/Back River cottages. The Raised Tybee Cottage retains the square shape, two story height, and recessed wraparound porch of the South End/Back River Cottages while employing the basic functionality of the Strand Cottage: the open, raised ground level containing the servants' quarters and changing rooms with exterior lattice surround. The combination of the compact square shape of the South End/Back River Cottages and the ground level location of the changing rooms and servants' quarters of the Strand Cottages allowed maximum utilization of the newly subdivided lots. The most significant evolutionary trait of the Raised Tybee Cottage, however, is its full-height ground level, which was raised a full story in order to incorporate garage space for automobiles. Because Tybee's streets were little more than one lane sand pathways when these seaside cottages were built, it was necessary to provide a place to store the automobiles of the new generation of summer cottage owners without using up more of the already space-challenged lots.

With this in mind, it is apparent that the compact design of the Raised Tybee Cottage and its accommodation of the automobile are local characteristics that reflect the changes in land use and development trends brought on by the completion of the Tybee Road. It appears that the cottage type was introduced shortly after the opening of Tybee Road and the design was subsequently adopted by Tybee's cottage builders. By the early 1930s the Raised Tybee Cottage had become a local building standard for beach houses on Tybee.

Although the design of the Raised Tybee Cottage is not attributed to any one builder or architect, A. P. Solomon Jr., owner of the Tybee Contracting Company, is probably the most closely associated with the genesis and construction of this unique beach cottage type. In 1931 Solomon established Shirley Park Subdivision between Butler Avenue and the ocean and between 10th and Shirley Streets. Built adjacent the Fresh Air Home, the development was billed in newspaper advertisements as "Tybee's New and Only Ocean Front Subdivision." While most speculators and developers were selling off subdivided lots one by one to individuals, Solomon offered lots and cottages "built and sold as a unit." Created through the subdivision of two original oceanfront lots, the Shirley Park Subdivision offered 17 graded building lots with electric and water connections. Solomon's contribution to the development of the Raised Tybee cottage is evidenced in the building plans offered by his company to individuals purchasing lots in Shirley Park. As pointed out in an advertisement for the subdivision that appeared in the May 17, 1931 edition of the *Savannah Morning News*, Solomon was offering prospective buyers "several plans which he has and which his company will build and sell to purchasers, complete." Of the 15 cottages built by Solomon and his company in Shirley Park, 11 are Raised Tybee Cottages. In addition to these, several Raised Tybee Cottages built before and after 1931 have been attributed to Solomon and the Tybee Contracting Company, leaving little doubt that Solomon was, at the very least, a leading proponent of the design on Tybee.

Raised cottages were built throughout the remainder of the 1930s, with variations of the type persisting through the 1940s and 1950s. Although the cottages were originally built on lots on the ocean side of Butler Avenue, by the mid 1930s Raised Tybee Cottages were being built on smaller lots throughout the island. With most of the seaside lots no longer available, the compact size of the Raised Tybee Cottage was ideal for the small lots between Butler and Jones Avenues. By this time several variations of the Raised Tybee Cottage were introduced. Most variations involved the raised main living quarters, with the characteristics of the ground level remaining intact. The most popular variation involved the introduction of the bungalow plan to the equation, essentially creating a "raised bungalow." While these variations moved away from the square form, hip roofs, and recessed wrap-around porches associated with the early Raised Tybee Cottages, the spirit of the type is maintained through the retention of the ground level, which still included servant quarters, bath/changing room, auto stalls, and a lattice work surround.

Today, the Raised Tybee Cottage is recognized by architectural historians and preservationists as a unique local building type, with regional and national authorities conceding that the cottage is an outstanding example of coastal summer resort architecture that appears to be found only on Tybee Island. Existing scholarship confirms that these types of cottages are unique on the Georgia coast, being unlike the simple bungalows of St. Simons or the architect-designed cottages of Jekyll Island. The heavy influence of French Colonial architecture on the design of the Raised Tybee Cottage is readily evident, having been transplanted from the Caribbean and Mississippi Delta region by Tybee's builders. However, the builders' incorporation of twentieth century design specifications influenced by local events—the construction of Tybee Road and the necessary accommodation of the automobile—combined with eighteenth and nineteenth century Creole architectural traditions, lends support to the theory that the Raised Tybee Cottage, while not a totally original design, possesses features that appear to be unique in summer resort cottage architecture.

In 2004, an inventory of all historic resources on Tybee identified 110 examples of the Raised Tybee Cottage. Raised Tybee Cottages were identified as the most common historic building type on Tybee, representing nearly 25 percent of the historic resources remaining on the island. Through the leadership of the Tybee Island Historical Society, cottage owners and preservationists are raising awareness of the significance of these unique beach houses in an effort to list all of the island's Raised Tybee Cottages on the National Register of Historic Places.

HOTELS AND OTHER LODGINGS
(Names in italics denote building still intact.)

Hotels, Motels, and Inns

Hotel Bolton — Built in 1850s. Possibly extant: local accounts maintain moved from location near vicinity of lighthouse when Ft. Screven constructed.

Ocean House — Built in 1876 near 3rd Street. Destroyed by fire or hurricane *c.* 1891–1897.

Furber's Point House — Built near Ocean House in 1880s. Destroyed by hurricane *c.* 1893–1897.

Ocean View Hotel — Built near Ocean House in 1880s. Destroyed by hurricane 1893-1897.

Hotel Tybee (original) — Built on ocean between 14th and 15th Streets in 1891. Destroyed by fire in 1908.

South End Hotel — Built between Atlantic Avenue and 16th Street in 1890s. Non-extant by 1910, probably destroyed by fire.

Hotel Tybee (second) — Built on site of original in 1911. North wing remodeled into *Tybee Motel* in 1958. Center section and south wing demolished in 1961.

Sea Breeze Hotel — Built in 1910s along Atlantic Avenue. Hotel burned in 1963, restaurant extant.

Ocean View Hotel (second) — Built on corner of Butler Avenue and 16th Street in 1910s. Renamed the Mayflower Hotel in 1950s, still standing in 1960s.

Inlet Hotel — Built in1890s as the Tybee Inlet Club on the corner of Inlet Avenue and 17th Street. Used as a boarding house in 1910s and 1920s.

Atlantic Club Hotel — Built in 1880s as the Atlantic Club on the corner of Butler Avenue and 8th Street. Used as a boarding house 1920s–1930s.

Lindy Hotel — Built in 1925 on the corner of Butler and 15th Street, renamed the Savannah Beach Hotel in 1929. Destroyed by fire in 1931.

Solms Hotel — Built in 1932 on the corner of Strand and Izlar Avenue. Renamed the Sundowner Hotel in 1970s. Demolished for condo development in 2002.

Wilson Hotel — Built in 1930s on 16th Street between Butler and Strand. Remodeled for use as apartments in 1980s.

Strand Hotel — Built in 1930s on the corner of Inlet Avenue and Strand. Remodeled for use as a restaurant in 1950s.

Desoto Beach Hotel — Built *c.* 1940 as the Desoto Beach Hotel and Cabana Club on Butler Avenue and 3rd Street. Demolished in 1999 for condo development.

Tybee Terrace Cottages — Originally built in 1940s as the American Tourist Court on the corner of Butler Avenue and 7th Street. Several duplex cottages added *c.* 1950.

The Tides — 48 room, U-shaped motel court built in 1950s on the inland side of Butler between 14th and 15th Streets. Demolished in 2000 for Best Western.

The Waves — U-shaped motel court built in early 1950s on original site of the Lindy Hotel (inland side of Butler at 15th Street). Demolished in 2000 for new motel.

The Blair Apartments — An eight unit auto court built in 1940s consisting of two parallel frame one story buildings. Rodeway Inn located on site.

The Royal Palms Motel — Two story motel court built in 1960s on the inland side of Butler Avenue between 9th and 10th Streets.

The Verandah Motel — Built in 1960s on original Hotel Tybee site, oceanfront at the corner of 15th Street and Strand. Demolished in 1990s to build present Ocean Plaza Resort.

Islander Motel and Apts. — Built in early 1970s on the corner of Butler and Silver Avenue. Now Tango Inn.

Days Inn — Built on corner of Butler Avenue and 14th Street in 1970. First unit of what later became the Days Inn chain. Now called the Sand Castle Inn.

The Seagull — Motel Court built in 1960s on the inland side of Butler Avenue at 15th Street. Still in operation as the Happy Holiday Motel.

Belair Motel — Built in 1970s on the inland side of Butler Avenue on site of Blair Apartments. Demolished for Rodeway Inn.

Ramada Inn by the Sea — Built 1971 on the ocean side of Butler Avenue between 3rd and 4th Streets.

The Sands Motel — Built *c.* 1960s as The New Ocean Terrace Motel on part of the original Hotel Tybee site. Burned down in 1992.

Ocean Plaza Hotel — Large two building, three-story hotel built along ocean front strand in 1990s on original site of Hotel Tybee between 14th and 15th Streets.

Super 8 Motel — Built in 1999 on the former site of the Easton Ride Center/Tybee Island Amusement Center on 16th Street. Now called the Sea Breeze Inn.

Howard Johnson — Built in 2000 on the site of the Waves Motel, corner of Butler Avenue and 15th Street.

Rodeway Inn — Built on the site of the Belair Motel on Butler between 9th and 10th.

Best Western — Built in 2000s on site of the Tides Motel, inland side of Butler between 15th and 16th Streets. Now called the Dunes Motel.

Apartments and Boarding Houses

Bynum's Riverside House — Built *c.* 1900 on the Back River, corner of Chatham and Alley 2. Used as a summer cottage, the Collins Cottage, 1920–1993. Destroyed by fire in 1996.

Curry House — Boarding house built in 1900s along Izlar Avenue. One of 20 buildings destroyed by the fire of 1931.

Caldwell House — Boarding house built in 1900s along Izlar Avenue. One of 20 buildings destroyed by the fire of 1931.

Anton Solm's Seaside Cottages — Two frame, two-story rental cottages built in 1910s at corner of Izlar Avenue and Strand. Origin of 1931 fire that destroyed 20 buildings. Solms Hotel built on site 1932.

Izlar's Boarding House — Built in 1910s on Izlar Avenue between Butler and Strand.

Barbee's Beach Haven Apartments — Boarding house district on 17th Street between Butler and ocean. Originally built in 1910s as a summer cottage, Blumberg Cottage, and converted into a boarding house in 1930s. Burned down in 1987.

The Oleander — Boarding house district on 17th Street between Butler and the ocean. Originally built in 1910s as a summer cottage, Roberts Cottage, converted into a boarding house in 1930s. Destroyed by fire in 1987.

Cobb Apartments — Originally a summer cottage built in 1900s, Pindar Cottage, on corner of 17th Street and Strand. Remodeled as a boarding house in 1930s. Heart of boarding house district by 1970s, having absorbed the Andris Apartments on opposite corner of 17th Street. Four building complex demolished to build condos in 1997.

Blumenthal House — Built as a boarding house in 1910s on 17th Street between Butler and ocean. Operated as the Sheppard Apartments as late as the 1970s.

Beach View Apartments — Originally built as a summer cottage in 1910s, Boardley Cottage, on inland corner of Butler and 17th Street. Remodeled as boarding house in 1930s. Operated today as the Hunter House Inn and Restaurant.

Riverside Lodge — Built in 1928 on Chatham Avenue overlooking the Back River. Used as a fishing camp through the 1960s. Private summer cottage today.

Georgianna Inn — Originally built as a summer cottage in 1910s, Cummings Cottage, ocean side of Butler Avenue between 14th and 13th Streets. Remodeled as a boarding house in 1921.

Carbo House — After original building (built 1925) was destroyed by the fire of 1931, this frame, two-story, 16 room boarding house was built in 1932 on the same site. Still operated as a boarding house.

Sea View Apartments — Originally built as a summer cottage in 1930s on 18th Street between Butler and ocean. Converted for use as apartments in 1950s.

Powers Apartment Building — Built as a boarding house in 1930s on 17th Street between Butler and ocean.

Andris Apartments — Two-unit, concrete block apartment complex built on corner of 17th Street and Strand in 1930s. Later part of Cobb Apartment complex, demolished in 1997.

May's Apartments — Two-story brick apartment building built in 1937 near corner of Butler and 16th Street. Two commercial storefronts and four apartments.

TIMELINE OF SIGNIFICANT
HISTORICAL EVENTS

1520 — Lucas Vasquez de Ayllon explores the east coast of America, claiming for Spain the area from the Bahamas to Nova Scotia, later called La Florida by the Spanish.

1540 — Hernando De Soto explores what is today the southeastern United States, encounters the Guale of coastal Georgia.

1565 — Pedro Menendez de Aviles establishes St. Augustine, the first permanent European settlement in North America.

1566 — Menendez establishes a chain of missions along the Atlantic coast from St. Augustine to Santa Elena on Parris Island, South Carolina.

1605–1670 — Thousands of Guale Indians are converted to Christianity by Franciscan friars during the "golden age" of Spanish missions in Georgia.

1670 — Charles Towne established in Carolina, beginning of English encroachment into Spanish Georgia.

1680 — The Mission de Santa Catalina de Guale abandoned following fierce attack by 300 English-led Yamasee Indians.

1683–1685 — English forces from Charles Towne conduct a series of destructive raids on remaining coastal missions.

1686 — Final withdrawal of Spanish missionaries from Georgia.

1733 — Oglethorpe founds colony of Georgia. A short-lived settlement is established on Tybee as a frontier outpost.

1736 — John Wesley arrives with Oglethorpe off the coast of Tybee, first sets foot on American soil at Estill Hammock.

1736 — First "lighthouse," a daymark, is established on Tybee under the direction of Noble Jones.

1742 — A second daymark is constructed to replace the first, which was swept away by a storm.

1768 — A quarantine station, called the Lazaretto (Italian for "pest house"), is established at the west end of Tybee.

1773 — A third lighthouse is constructed, replacing the existing daymark, which was in danger of being washed away by the tides. Lit by spermaceti candles, this is Tybee's first true lighthouse.

1776 — Beginning of Revolutionary War, Tory settlement established on Tybee.

1778 — First capture of a British vessel by an American-commissioned warship occurs off Tybee.

1778 — British establish Fort Tybee, a small sand fort, on the North End of the island near the lighthouse.

1779 — During the weeks preceding the Siege of Savannah, Tybee serves as a major staging area for the French fleet, one of the largest gatherings of foreign ships every assembled off the coast of the United States.

1815 — Isaiah Davenport commissioned by the U.S. government to construct a martello tower on the beach near the lighthouse to guard the entrance to the Savannah River.

1861 — Tybee abandoned by Confederate troops. Union army occupies Tybee Island, lighthouse established as headquarters for the siege of Fort Pulaski.

1862 — Raiding party of the Montgomery Guards from Fort Pulaski destroy a major portion of the Tybee Lighthouse by igniting a keg of powder on the third floor.

1862 — Federal batteries constructed along the east coast of Tybee. Siege and reduction of Fort Pulaski marks the first effective use of rifled cannon against a masonry fortification, rendering these types of defenses obsolete.

1867 — Tybee Lighthouse rebuilt utilizing the lower 60 feet of the 1773 tower. The new 150 foot tall, masonry and metal tower is equipped with a first-order Fresnel lens.

1873 — Tybee Improvement Company established to develop island into a resort, partial survey of island into building lots commissioned.

1875 — 210 acres are acquired by the federal government on the North End of Tybee for the establishment of a military reservation.

1876 — Ocean House, the first resort hotel built on Tybee, is completed on the South End of the island across from the present Town Hall.

1881–1882 — Tybee incorporated as the town of Ocean City, changed the following year to the town of Tybee.

1885 — Tybee Beach Company gains controlling interest in island.

1887 — Savannah-Tybee Railroad completed.

1891 — Hotel Tybee completed on South End of Island.

1893 — Massive hurricane devastates island, 80 percent of buildings destroyed.

1895 — Tybee becomes a regional resort when the Savannah-Tybee Railroad becomes a unit of the Central of Georgia Railroad.

1897 — In preparation for the Spanish-American War, Fort Screven is established on the North End of Tybee as an army coast artillery station.

1900 — Central of Georgia builds the Tybrisa Pavilion near Hotel Tybee on the South End.

1908 — Hotel Tybee destroyed by fire.

1911 — A new three-and-a-half story, concrete hotel is built on the site of the original Hotel Tybee. New hotel is completed in time for the opening of the 1911 season.

1914 — Martello Tower destroyed by U.S. Army Corp of Engineers to provide a clear field of fire for Fort Screven's guns.

1923 — Tybee Road completed, Tybee begins golden era as a resort.

1924 — Fort Screven established as the headquarters of the 8th Infantry Regiment.

1925 — Tybee Beach Company establishes Venetian Terrace Subdivision.

1929 — "Ocean parkway" established between 14th and 17th Streets along Strand. Name changed to city of Savannah Beach.

1931 — Fire destroys 20 buildings in boarding house district along Strand, firemen and volunteers successfully prevent fire from spreading to oceanfront resort center.

1932 — Lt. Colonel George Marshall assumes his first post, command at Fort Screven.

1933 — Central of Georgia discontinues train service to Tybee.

1938–1939 — WPA projects result in the construction of concrete parking pavilions, concrete seawall, and "ocean walkway" between 14th and 18th Streets along the Strand, as well as the construction of the existing Tybee City Hall.

1940 — The Desoto Beach Hotel and Cabana Club, the last major hostelry built on Tybee, is completed near the original site of the Ocean House.

1941 — Fort Screven established as a training command center for the U.S. Corps of Engineers Deep Sea Diving and Salvage School, the army's only training facility for beginning divers, at a site near Chimney Creek.

1944–1946 — Fort Screven declared surplus, property and buildings dispensed to the city through the Federal Housing Administration. Fort Screven Development Company formed to offer property and buildings for sale to public.

1947 — The Desoto Beach Hotel and Cabana Club serves as one of three host sites for the International Monetary Conference. Based in Savannah, the conference is the inaugural meeting of the international organization that later became the World Bank.

1954–1955 — Unparalleled boom in the construction of year-round homes continues at Savannah Beach with the establishment of the Palm Terrace Subdivision along Lewis Avenue and Holiday Park Subdivision at Spanish Hammock.

1958 — North wing of Hotel Tybee converted for use as a 22-room motel.

1961 — As part of plans to redevelop site, central section and south wing of Hotel Tybee demolished.

1961 — Tybee Museum established in Battery Garland as a resort attraction.

1964 — Islands Expressway opens, providing direct route between downtown Savannah and Tybee.

1967 — Tybee loses its historic oceanfront resort center when its remaining resort attraction, the Tybrisa Pavilion and Bathhouse Building, is destroyed by a major fire that ravaged it and other oceanfront structures along the Strand between 15th and 16th Streets.

1970 — Days Inn established at corner of Butler Avenue and 14th Street, the first unit of what would become the Days Inn hotel and motel chain.

1978 — Savannah Beach changes name back to the city of Tybee Island.

1981 — The island's first major condominium project, Tybee Ocean Villas, is completed along the Strand between 15th and 16th Street where the Tybrisa Bathhouse and the Brass Rail had been located.

1981 — Fort Screven Historic District listed on National Register of Historic Places.

1986 — Tybee Museum Association changes name to Tybee Island Historical Society to reflect expanded role of managing both the Tybee Museum and the Tybee Lighthouse.

1996 — Tybee Pavilion built on site of Tybrisa.

1996 — The sailing event of the Centennial Olympic Games held in Savannah sparks renewed interest in Tybee.

1995–1999 — Olympics and construction of new pavilion initiates an unprecedented building boom, historic summer cottages, small hotels, and boarding houses are demolished at an alarming rate to make way for oceanfront condominiums.

1999 — Tybee Island Strand Cottages and Tybee Island Back River Historic Districts listed on National Register of Historic Places.

1999 — The Desoto Beach Hotel is demolished for new hotel/condominium project despite public protests. Loss galvanizes an already active preservation movement to work toward the preservation of the island's unique coastal architecture.

1999 — Tybee Island Historical Society begins a four phase restoration of the Light Station that will culminate in the restoration of the lighthouse and its three historic keeper's cottages.

2004 — Department of the Interior transfers ownership of the Tybee Light Station to the Tybee Island Historical Society, the first recipient of the Lighthouse Transfer Program in the nation.

BIBLIOGRAPHY

Adams, James Mack. *A History of Fort Screven, Georgia: Tybee Island's Military Heritage.* Tybee Island: JMA2 Publications, 1996.

Aiken, Conrad. "Strange Moonlight." *Literary Savannah.* Athens, Georgia: Hill Street Press, 1998.

Chatham County Historic Resources Survey, 1992–1993 conducted by the Chatham County Metropolitan Planning Commission, Savannah.

Ciucevich, Robert A. *Raised Tybee Cottage Multiple Property National Register Registration Form.* Tybee Island: On file at the Historic Preservation Division, Georgia Department of Natural Resources, Atlanta, 2005.

————. *Tybee Island Strand Cottages National Register Historic District Nomination.* Tybee Island: On file at the Historic Preservation Division, Georgia Department of Natural Resources, Atlanta, 1997.

————. *Tybee Island Back River National Register Historic District Nomination.* Tybee Island: On file at the Historic Preservation Division, Georgia Department of Natural Resources, Atlanta, 1997.

————. *Tybee Island Historic Resources Survey Report.* Savannah: Quatrefoil Consulting, 2004.

Coleman, Kenneth, ed. *A History of Georgia.* Athens, Georgia: The University of Georgia Press, 1977.

Estill, J. H. "Tales of Tybee." *Savannah Morning News,* Feb 12, 1905.

Gamble, Thomas. *Savannah Duels and Duelists.* Savannah: Review Publishing and Printing Company, 1923.

Godley, Margaret. *Historic Tybee Island.* Savannah: Savannah Beach Chamber of Commerce, 1958.

Guss, John Walker. *Fortresses of Savannah, Georgia.* Charleston, South Carolina: Arcadia Publishing, 2002.

Hervey, Harry *The Damned Don't Cry.* 1939

Fort Screven National Register Historic District Nomination. Tybee Island: Richard Cloues (HPD). On file at the Historic Preservation Division, Georgia Department of Natural Resources, Atlanta, 1980.

Jones, Charles C. Jr., ed. *The Siege of Savannah by the Fleet of Count D'Estaing in 1779.* New York: The *New York Times* and the Arno Press, 1968.

Lattimore, Ralston B. "Fort Pulaski National Monument: National Park Service Historical Handbook Series No. 18." Washington, D.C.: U.S. Government Printing Office, 1954.

Lawrence, Alexander A. *A Present For Mr. Lincoln: The Story of Savannah from Succession to Sherman.* Macon, Georgia: The Ardivan Press, 1961.

Miller, Cynthia A. *Tybee Island, Ga.: Changing Images and Land Uses, 1733–1895.* Presented at the Eastern Historical Geography Association Annual Meeting, Savannah, October 1986.

Piechocinski, Elizabeth Carpenter. *Once Upon an Island.* Savannah: The Oglethorpe Press, 2003.

Richardson, B. H. *A History of Tybee Island, Ga., and a Sketch of the Savannah and Tybee Railroad.* Savannah: Savannah Times Publishing Company, 1886.

Sieg, Edward Chan. *Eden on the Marsh: An Illustrated History of Savannah.* Northridge, California: Windsor Publications, 1985.

Southern Scenes . . . Points and Pictures along the Central of Georgia Railway. Buffalo, New York: The Matthews-Northrup Co., 1897

Stovall, Pleasant A. *Fruits of Industry: Points and Pictures along the Central Railroad of Georgia.* Buffalo, New York: The Matthews-Northrup Co., 1895.

Thomas, David Hurst. *St. Catherines: An Island in Time.* Atlanta: Endowment for the Humanities, 1988.

Varnedoe, Sam L. *Memoirs of Tybee Island: 1909–1988.* Tybee Island: 1988.

Newspaper and Magazine Articles

"The Ancient Martello Tower." The *New York Herald*, 1862.

"Beach Club Owners Deplore Gambling Ban, Pastor Hails It." *Savannah Morning News*, April 18, 1963, 1.

"Beach Reports Building Boom." *Savannah Morning News*, February 24, 1946, 28.

"Bus Service Replaces Steam Trains on Tybee District." *Central of Georgia Magazine*, November 1930, 11.

"A Cyclone of Death." *Savannah Morning News*, August 29, 1893, 1.

Carroll, John. "Roaring Flames Destroy Block of Tybee Strand." *Savannah Morning News*, May 17, 1967.

"Distant Tybee." *Savannah Evening Press*, February 10, 1933.

Duncan, John. "Island soothes tired, troubled visitors." *Inside Savannah*, June 1985, 22-26.

"Fire Protection Planned at Tybee." *Savannah Morning News*, July 29, 1931, 12.

Gamble, Thomas. "Memories of Savannah's Greatest Hurricane Fifty Years Ago Recalled." *Savannah Morning News*, August 22, 1943.

Gamble, Thomas. "Savannah Beach has Plans to Develop Along Large Lines." *Savannah Morning News*, June, 28, 1931.

Gillon, Alan, "Beach Told Machines Must Go." *Savannah Morning News*, April, 18, 1963, 1.

Gunderson, Arthur. "Tybee 'days of glory.'" *Savannah News-Press Magazine*, February 1, 1970, 8–9.

Gunderson, Arthur. "Tybee . . . The Days of the Big Bands." *Savannah News-Press Magazine*, February 15, 1970, 6–7.

"Historic Tybee Island." *Savannah Morning News*, May 28, 1888.

"Improvement Plans at Savannah Beach Will Put it in Front Rank." *Savannah Morning News*, September 1, 1929, 10.

"Judge Bacon Speaks at Rotary Meeting: Says Tybee Road Cost County $1,192,766.59." *Savannah Morning News*, June 20, 1923.

Keating, Mary, "Bids on Beach Toll Route to be Called For Within 70 Days." *Savannah Morning News*, March 20, 1959.

Lambright, Joseph E. "Shameful Conditions Demand Action." *Savannah Morning News*, September 3, 1957, 1-6.

Mallia, John. "Beach May Buy Hotel or Motel." *Savannah Morning News*, January 1, 1964, 8B.

Mathews, Bob. "Several Beach Buildings Destroyed: 16-Year Old Boy is Held In Connection With Fire." *Savannah Morning News*, September 17, 1967.

"New Brick Hotel For Tybee Island." *Savannah Morning News*, February 28, 1932, 1.

"New Hotel Tybee Formally Opened." *Savannah Morning News*, June 2, 1911.

"Oceanfront Property Sold: Entertainment Area Planned at Beach." *Savannah Morning News*, January 1, 1964, Section 1-8B.

"Official Opening At Savannah Beach Runs off Smoothly." *Savannah Morning News*, May 12, 1949, 22.

"Opening Set Today at Savannah Beach." *The* (Atlanta) *Constitution*, May 20, 1939.

Palmer, Kenneth. "Tybrisa Properties Sold to New Firm." *Savannah Evening Press*, September 3, 1964.

"Parking Space at Savannah Beach to be Most Attractive." *Savannah Morning News*, May 16, 1931, 18.

Puckett, Tom. "Tybee: Exclusive Elegance Now Family Fun." *Inside Savannah*, June 1985, 17-2.

"Razing Buildings is Check on Fire: Second Savannah Beach Fire in Last Few Weeks." *Savannah Morning News*, September 2, 1931, 14.

Rippen, Charles. "Tybee." *Coastal Quarterly*, Summer 1977, 38–44.

"Savannah Beach Formally Opens." *Savannah Morning News*, May 30, 1937, 16, 23.

Savannah Beach Officially Opens Season Today." *Savannah Morning News*, April 30, 1955, 2-13.

"Savannah Beach Opens New Season Wednesday With Attractions of All Kinds Along Its Ocean Front." *Savannah Morning News*, May 17, 1931, 4A.

"Sees Evolution of Bathing Suit at Tybee and Decline of Picnickers and Mosquitoes." *Savannah Evening Press*, April 17, 1931.

Sellers, Beryl, "Beach Road Takes Shape." *Savannah Morning News*, May 3, 1963.

"Seventieth Year as Resort Center." *Savannah Evening Press*, May 23, 1940, 12.

"Sheriff Declares War on Chatham Gambling." *Savannah Morning News*, April 16, 1963, 1.

"The Siege and Capture of Fort Pulaski." *Frank Leslie's Illustrated Newspaper*, 1862, 285.

"The South Coast Martello Towers," www.martello-towers.co.uk.

Stovall, Pleasant A. "The Cyclone In The South." *Harper's Weekly*, September 16, 1893.

"Surrender of Fort Pulaski," *New York Daily Tribune*, April 19, 1862.

"Thousands Today Hit Rubber Tires Toward Sea—Victory Drive, Tybee Highway Route, Dream at Last Realized," *Savannah Morning News*, March 21, 1923.

"Twenty Buildings Burn at Savannah Beach as High Winds Fan Flames." *Savannah Morning News*, July 22, 1931, 2, 14.

"Tybee Group To Build 60 Bungalows," *Savannah Morning News*, January 24, 1954, 3-24.

Tybee Hotel and Improvement Company, "Tybee Island: The Playground of the Southeast." Savannah: Review Publishing & Printing Co., 1926.

"Tybee Hotel Gets Ready for 'Tunnel.'" *Savannah Morning News*, January 19, 1962.

"Tybee Island, Savannah's Popular Summer Resort," *Savannah Morning News*, September 6, 1888.

"Tybee Isle Museum Planned by Savannah Beach Chamber," *Savannah Evening Press*, September 4, 1958.

"Tybee Museum Draws Over 8,000 Visitors," *Savannah Evening Press*, September 2, 1961.

"Tybee—Our Summer Resort," *Savannah Morning News*, March 2, 1877.

Whitfield, Archie. "Historical Buildings Ravaged," *Savannah Morning News*, May 17, 1967.

INDEX